3302452309

40 Short Walks in

BA
714

BANBURY
MARLBOR
BANBURY
TEL. BANBURY 262282

To renew this book, phone 0845 1202811 or visit
our website at www.libcat.oxfordshire.gov.uk
You will need your library PIN number
(available from your library)

OXFORDSHIRE COUNTY COUNCIL
SOCIAL & COMMUNITY SERVICES
www.oxfordshire.gov.uk

Produced by AA Publishing
© AA Media Limited 2011

Researched and written by
Andrew McCloy

Additional material and walks by John
Gillham, Hugh Taylor and Moira McCrossan
(updated by Andrew McCloy)

Commissioning Editor: David Popey
Series Management: Sandy Draper
Series Design: Tracey Butler
Copy-editor: Pam Stagg
Proofreader: Chris Bagshaw
Picture Researcher: Lesley Grayson
Internal Repro and Image Manipulation:
Sarah Montgomery
Cartography provided by the Mapping
Services Department of AA Publishing
Production: Lorraine Taylor

Published by AA Publishing (a trading name
of AA Media Limited, whose registered office
is Fanum House, Basing View, Basingstoke,
Hampshire RG21 4EA; registered number
06112600)

All rights reserved. This publication or any
part of it may not be copied or reproduced
by any means without the prior permission
of the publisher. All inquiries should be
directed to the publisher.

  This product
includes mapping
data licensed from the Ordnance Survey®
with the permission of the Controller of
Her Majesty's Stationery Office. © Crown
Copyright 2011. All rights reserved.
Licence number 100021153.

A04616

978-0-7495-6907-5
978-0-7495-6919-8 (SS)

A CIP catalogue record for this book is
available from the British Library.

The contents of this book are believed
correct at the time of printing. Nevertheless,
the publishers cannot be held responsible
for any errors or omissions or for changes
in the details given in this book or for
the consequences of any reliance on the
information it provides. This does not affect
your statutory rights. We have tried to
ensure accuracy in this book, but things do
change and we would be grateful if readers
would advise us of any inaccuracies they
may encounter.

We have taken all reasonable steps to ensure
that these walks are safe and achievable
by walkers with a realistic level of fitness.
However, all outdoor activities involve a
degree of risk and the publishers accept
no responsibility for any injuries caused to
readers whilst following these walks. For
more advice on walking safely see page 144.
The mileage range shown on the front cover
is for guidance only – some walks may be
less than or exceed these distances.

Some of the walks may appear in other AA
books and publications.

Picture credits
The Automobile Association would like
to thank the following photographers,
companies and picture libraries for their
assistance in the preparation of this book.

3 AA/T Mackie; 7 AA/A Midgley; 10 AA/A J
Hopkins; 20 AA/N Coates; 30 AA/T Mackie;
40 AA/M Birkitt; 53 AA/M Birkitt; 60/61
steven gillis hd9 imaging/Alamy; 74 david
martyn hughes/Alamy; 81 AA/M Birkitt; 100
AA/T Mackie; 110 AA/T Mackie; 123 AA/T
Mackie; 134 AA/T Mackie; 140 AA/T Mackie

Every effort has been made to trace the
copyright holders, and we apologise in
advance for any accidental errors. We would
be happy to apply the corrections in the
following edition of this publication.

AA

40 Short Walks in

THE PEAK DISTRICT

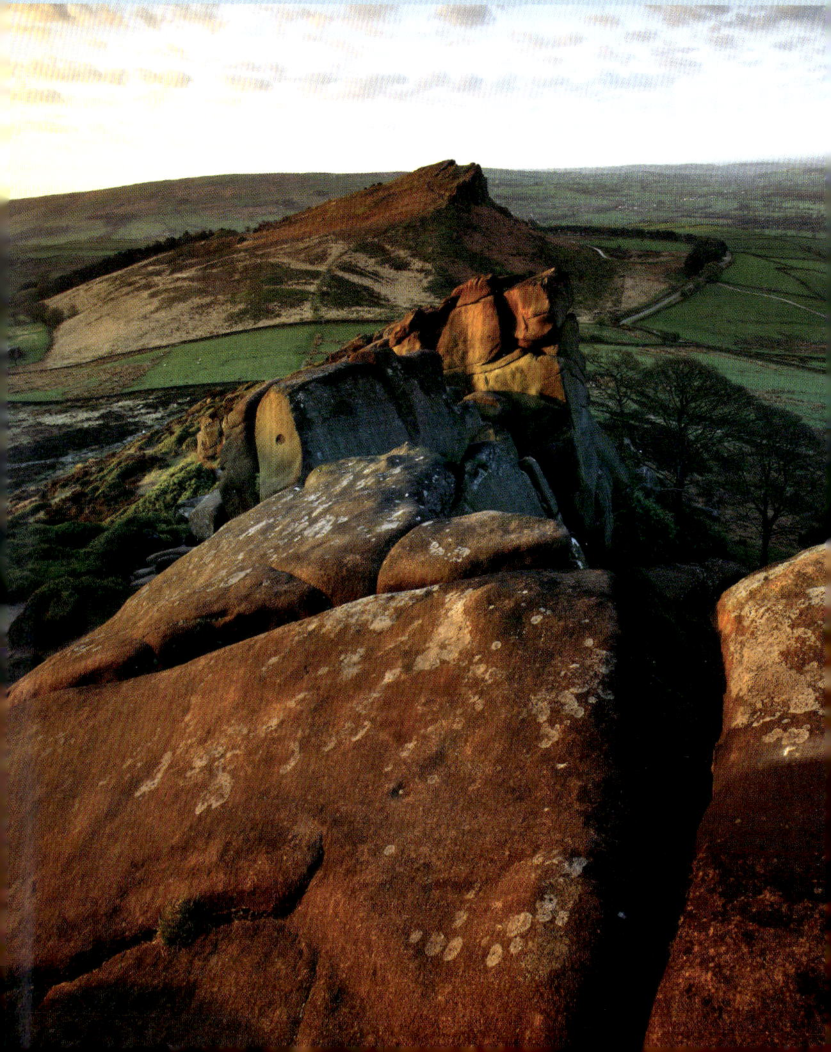

Contents

Walk		Rating	Distance	Page
1	Langsett	✚✚✚	2.75 miles (4.4km)	10
2	Dovestone	✚✚✚	2.25 miles (3.6km)	14
3	New Mills	✚✚✚	1 mile (1.6km)	17
4	Hayfield	✚✚✚	4 miles (6.4km)	21
5	Woodlands Valley	✚✚✚	1.25 miles (2km)	24
6	Edale	✚✚✚	3.75 miles (6km)	27
7	Win Hill	✚✚✚	4 miles (6.4km)	31
8	Rivelin & Redmires	✚✚✚	4 miles (6.4km)	34
9	Lyme Park	✚✚✚	2 miles (3.2km)	37
10	Taxal & Fernilee Reservoir	✚✚✚	3.5 miles (5.7km)	41
11	Combs Reservoir	✚✚✚	3 miles (4.8km)	44
12	Hay Dale	✚✚✚	1.5 miles (2.4km)	47
13	Castleton	✚✚✚	3.5 miles (5.7km)	50
14	Bretton Clough	✚✚✚	2.5 miles (4km)	54
15	Padley Gorge	✚✚✚	3 miles (4.8km)	57
16	Eyam	✚✚✚	1 mile (1.6km)	62
17	Baslow Edge	✚✚✚	1.75 miles (2.8km)	65
18	Linacre Reservoirs	✚✚✚	2.75 miles (4.4km)	68
19	Beeley	✚✚✚	4 miles (6.4km)	71
20	Longstone Edge	✚✚✚	2.5 miles (4km)	75
21	Sheldon & Magpie Mine	✚✚✚	1.25 miles (2km)	78
22	Chelmorton & Deep Dale	✚✚✚	3.5 miles (5.7km)	82
23	Buxton	✚✚✚	2 miles (3.2km)	85
24	Goyt Valley	✚✚✚	3.5 miles (5.7km)	88

Walk	Rating	Distance	Page
25 Bollington	✚✚	3.5 miles (5.7km)	91
26 Tegg's Nose	✚✚	2.5 miles (4km)	94
27 Three Shire Heads	✚✚	4 miles (6.4km)	97
28 Lud's Church	✚✚	3.25 miles (5.3km)	101
29 Earl Sterndale & High Wheeldon	✚✚	2.75 miles (4.4km)	104
30 Youlgreave & Bradford Dale	✚	2 miles (3.2km)	107
31 Lathkill Dale	✚✚	3.25 miles (5.3km)	111
32 Stanton Moor	✚✚	4 miles (6.4km)	114
33 Matlock & Derwent Valley	✚✚	2.5 miles (4km)	117
34 Cromford	✚✚	3.5 miles (5.7km)	120
35 Wirksworth	✚	1.5 miles (2.4km)	124
36 Minninglow	✚	3 miles (4.8km)	127
37 Tissington	✚	3 miles (4.8km)	130
38 Dovedale	✚	2 miles (3.2km)	133
39 Ecton	✚✚✚	4 miles (6.4km)	137
40 Grindon	✚✚	3.5 miles (5.7km)	141

Rating
Each walk is rated for its relative difficulty compared to the other walks in this book. Walks marked ✚ are likely to be shorter and easier with little total ascent. The hardest walks are marked ✚✚✚

Walking in Safety
For advice and safety tips see page 144.

Introduction

If there is one word that sums up the enormous pull of walking in the Peak District National Park it's 'variety'. To start with there's the well-known White Peak/Dark Peak divide, with the southern half of the region underpinned by pearly white limestone, which manifests itself in delectable grassy dales and rolling pasture intersected by miles of dry-stone walls. To the north is the higher, harsher Dark Peak, where gritstone moorland topped by peat signals the beginning of the Pennine chain. Like white and dark chocolate, some prefer one over the other. Then there are the different faces of the Peak. The south-west aspect (the Staffordshire moorlands) looks and feels totally different from the Derbyshire dales in the south-east, which is different again from the high and remote Pennine uplands of the far north (Oldham and West Yorkshire) or the rounded heather moors above Chesterfield and Sheffield in the east.

Walking Opportunities
This contrast is reflected in the range of walking opportunities that the Peak District presents. Part of its appeal is that there is something for everyone. These short walks prove, if it were really necessary, that you don't have to walk hard or far to experience sublime scenery or features of interest. Sure, you can opt for an energetic moorland ascent or scale a hilltop, but in the Peak District this can be a relatively short and straightforward outing requiring mostly stamina and strong legs. But there are numerous walks exploring peaceful dales, rivers or unspoiled villages that are as enjoyable and rewarding as they are short and undemanding.

Spectacular Landscapes, Natural History and Plenty More
Several walks examine the Peak's spectacular natural landforms, such as dry limestone valleys, river gorges and high gritstone edges. The actual rock itself plays a key role, with the mining of lead and copper and the quarrying of limestone fashioning not just the landscape but the communities that grew up there. Water is also a recurring theme, from the rivers that drain out in all directions to the reservoirs built to quench the thirst of the urban communities that surround the Peak.

Many of the walks in this book touch on sites of previous human activity, from the sketchy remains of early settlers to the more obvious legacy of recent mining, mills and railways. You will see how, albeit gradually, the detrimental effects of heavy industries are being tempered as nature is

Opposite: View from Mam Tor near Castleton

helped to once again take hold. Indeed, it's not surprising that natural history figures highly in this book, and many of the walks look at aspects of the region's rich biodiversity, from butterflies and river birds to meadow flowers and stunning natural woodland.

Surprises in Britain's Oldest National Park

Most of the walks are located within the Peak District National Park, the oldest and still the most popular national park in the UK. Balancing conservation, recreation and economic interests is not always easy, as the Longstone Edge walk touches upon, but such a precious landscape needs safeguarding and the National Park is a body that deserves our full support.

Then there are all the surprises, and quite a few oddities, waiting just round the corner. Hilltop obelisks and follies, hidden chasms and caverns, ruined buildings and long lost industry, stone circles and railway crash pits, grand estates and paupers' cottages, weirdly-shaped rock outcrops and aerial walkways – all these and more are waiting to be discovered in *40 Short Walks in the Peak District*.

Using the Book

This collection of 40 walks is easy to use. Use the locator map to select your walk, then turn to the map and directions of your choice. The route of each walk is shown on a map and clear directions help you follow the walk. Each route is accompanied by background information about the walk and area.

INFORMATION PANELS
An information panel for each walk details the total distance, landscape, paths, parking, public toilets and any special conditions that apply, such as restricted access or level of dog friendliness. The minimum time suggested for the walk is for reasonably fit walkers and doesn't allow for stops.

ASCENT AND DIFFICULTY
An indication of the gradients you will encounter is shown by the rating ▲▲▲ (no steep slopes) to ▲▲▲ (several very steep slopes). Walks are also rated for difficulty. Walks marked ✚✚✚ are likely to be shorter and easier with little total ascent. The hardest walks are marked ✚✚✚.

MAPS AND START POINTS
There are 40 maps covering the walks. Some walks have a suggested option in the same area. Each walk has a suggested Ordnance Survey map. The start of each walk is given as a six-figure grid reference prefixed by two letters indicating which 100km square of the National Grid it refers to. You'll find more information on grid references on most Ordnance Survey maps.

CAR PARKING
Many of the car parks suggested are public, but occasionally you may find you have to park on the roadside or in a lay-by. Please be considerate when you leave your car, ensuring that access roads or gates are not blocked and that other vehicles can pass safely.

DOGS
We have tried to give dog owners useful advice about how dog friendly each walk is. Please respect other countryside users. Keep your dog under control, especially around livestock, and obey local bylaws and other dog control notices. Remember, it is against the law to let your dog foul in public areas, especially in villages and towns.

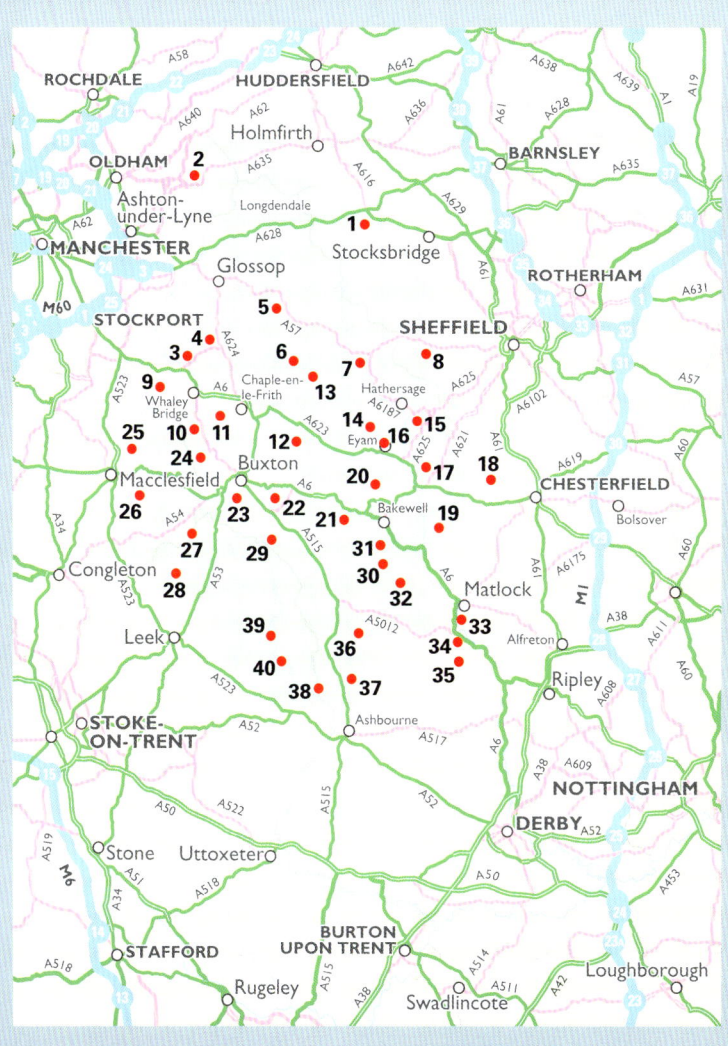

KEY TO WALKING MAPS

→→→	Walk Route		Built-up Area
①	Route Waypoint		Woodland Area
- - -	Adjoining Path	🚻	Toilet
☀	Viewpoint	P	Car Park
•	Place of Interest	⌐	Picnic Area
⌂	Steep Section	)(	Bridge

Using the Book 9

Langsett Walk 1

THE CHANGING FACE OF WATER

Langsett Reservoir now welcomes walkers and wildlife, a far cry from the old days.

The three reservoirs of Langsett, Midhope and Underbank were constructed in the final years of the 1800s to provide drinking water for the growing industrial communities of Sheffield, Barnsley, Doncaster and Rotherham. But to meet their needs sacrifices had to be made. Half-way around the walk you come to the former farmstead of Swinden, last inhabited in the 1930s. Like many other historic farms in the water catchment area for the newly built reservoirs, it was forcibly abandoned amid concerns that the precious water supplies might get contaminated.

Drovers' Tracks

The creation of Langsett Reservoir also meant changes to some historic routes, most notably the old drovers' track across the moors to Penistone market. Farmers used to drive their sheep and cattle from the Derwent Valley across the high moorland on a route known as Cut Gate, then down to Langsett and on to Penistone.

This walk is a little more modest, keeping to the wooded northern shores of Langsett Reservoir; but it also goes on to explore the mixed woods and farmland further west where several of the abandoned farms are located.

Woodland Habitat

At the start of the walk there are the usual conifer plantations, but as you will see by the paths and welcoming signs, Yorkshire Water's attitude is quite different today. Some of the wildlife-unfriendly plantations have been thinned and broadleaved varieties introduced. Indeed, on the south-western shores below North America Farm, most of the conifers are being replaced with birch and oak to create woodland habitats for birds such as warblers, flycatchers and woodpeckers. On the walk you will also pass a pond, in the woods near Swinden, which attracts wildlife such as newts, dragonflies and frogs; there's another near Brookhouse Bridge beyond the western end of the reservoir. Langsett Reservoir may still be about providing drinking water, but conservation and recreation are now part of the equation.

Opposite: View toward the reservoir at Langsett

Walk 1 Langsett

DISTANCE	MINIMUM TIME	GRADIENT	LEVEL OF DIFFICULTY
2.75 miles (4.4km)	1hr 30min	246ft (75m) ▲▲▲	✦✦✦

PATHS Firm woodland paths and farm tracks, one potentially muddy stretch
LANDSCAPE Upland reservoir fringed by woodland and high pasture
SUGGESTED MAP OS Explorer OL1 Dark Peak
START/FINISH Grid reference: SE 212004
DOG FRIENDLINESS Very good on woodland tracks, but on lead in sheep fields around Swinden
PARKING Langsett Barn car park **PUBLIC TOILETS** At car park

12 40 Short Walks in the Peak District

Langsett Walk 1

WALK 1 DIRECTIONS

❶ Leave the south-western corner of the car park through a fence gap by noticeboards. At the path junction take the second left, indicated public footpath, down an initially walled track (wall on your left) into the trees. At a fork go right and continue along this more or less level route high on the wooded slopes of Langsett Bank, ignoring all paths leading off.

❷ After a mile (1.6km) you come out at a wide cross track, with a short concrete strip underfoot. Go right, then in 275yds (251m) turn hard left on to a public bridleway signposted 'Swinden'.

❸ This track begins between old mossy walls then runs along the edge of the woods, with an open field on the right. Beyond a second gate turn left at the path junction to reach the site of the farmstead of Swinden.

❹ Turn left, opposite the large old barn, go through a gate and walk down a direct forest track, sometimes a little boggy in places. Go past a small pond, cross over a footbridge and then head up the grassy slope beyond to return to the concrete strip at Point ❷. Turn right and walk down the wide track for 75yds (69m).

❺ Turn left on to the signposted public footpath for a wide track that steadily descends through the trees towards the shores of the reservoir. Stay on this main track towards the bottom of the woods, with the water to your right.

❻ Eventually the reservoir dam and the rooftops of Langsett appear ahead. Ignore paths off to the left and instead go through a fence gap and at a junction take the second path on the left, indicated 'car park', to walk back up to the start. Before you head off home, it's worth pausing for a moment to admire refurbished Langsett Barn, which is around 400 years old.

🐾 IN THE AREA

North of Langsett the Trans Pennine Trail crosses the moors on its 215-mile (346km) coast-to-coast passage between Southport (Liverpool) and Hornsea (Hull). This walking/cycling/horse-riding route also has spurs to York, Leeds and Chesterfield, and you can sample a section from the car park and picnic site at Hazlehead or Dunford Bridge.

🍴 EATING AND DRINKING

Bank View Café is just a couple of minutes' walk away from the car park on the main road at Langsett. It's open every day, welcomes families and dogs, and in addition to the usual range of snacks and meals it has information on other local walks and stocks a range of guidebooks and outdoor equipment.

Walk 2: Dovestone

RATTLING THE POTS AND PANS

Two small peaks above Dovestone Reservoir offer great views and some interesting hilltop features.

Dovestone Reservoir, on the Peak District's north-western fringe above Oldham, is renowned for its moorland crags and rugged upland. On the western edge of the valley are some lower tops that offer equally invigorating outings, wide vistas and some curious hilltop decorations.

Pots and Pans

The first of the two objectives is shown as Board Hill on the Ordnance Survey map, although to many people it's more affectionately known as 'Pots and Pans' after the gritstone outcrop near the summit.

The other hilltop landmark that is visible for miles around is a tall stone obelisk, built in the last century to honour the local men who died in both World Wars. It was said to be sited so that it could be seen from the seven villages (Uppermill, Diggle, Dobcross, Greenfield, Lydgate, Springhead and Delph) that traditionally comprise Saddleworth. Every year a Remembrance service is held on this windy and exposed location of 1,400ft (427m). Indeed, the views from this lofty position are spectacular. Immediately below is a string of small communities that seem to run into each other – Uppermill, Greenfield, Grasscroft and Mossley – then over to the west, and partly hidden by Shaw Hill with its transmitter mast, is Oldham. To the south-west is the distant blur of Manchester, with its high-rise buildings.

Reservoirs

It's an easy moorland path across the rough but gently rising grassy slope to Alderman's Hill. However, as you reach the top you realise that the hill has a sterner side. Eastward-facing crags below the summit look sharply down to Dovestone and Yeoman Hey reservoirs in the valley bottom far below, as well as across to the line of crags on the edge of Saddleworth Moor.

The descent back to the car park is down the steep, grassy hillside along from the hilltop. It's no problem if taken slowly, or you can zig-zag down the slope since this is access land; but for a more straightforward return retrace your steps via Long Lane.

Dovestone

Walk 2

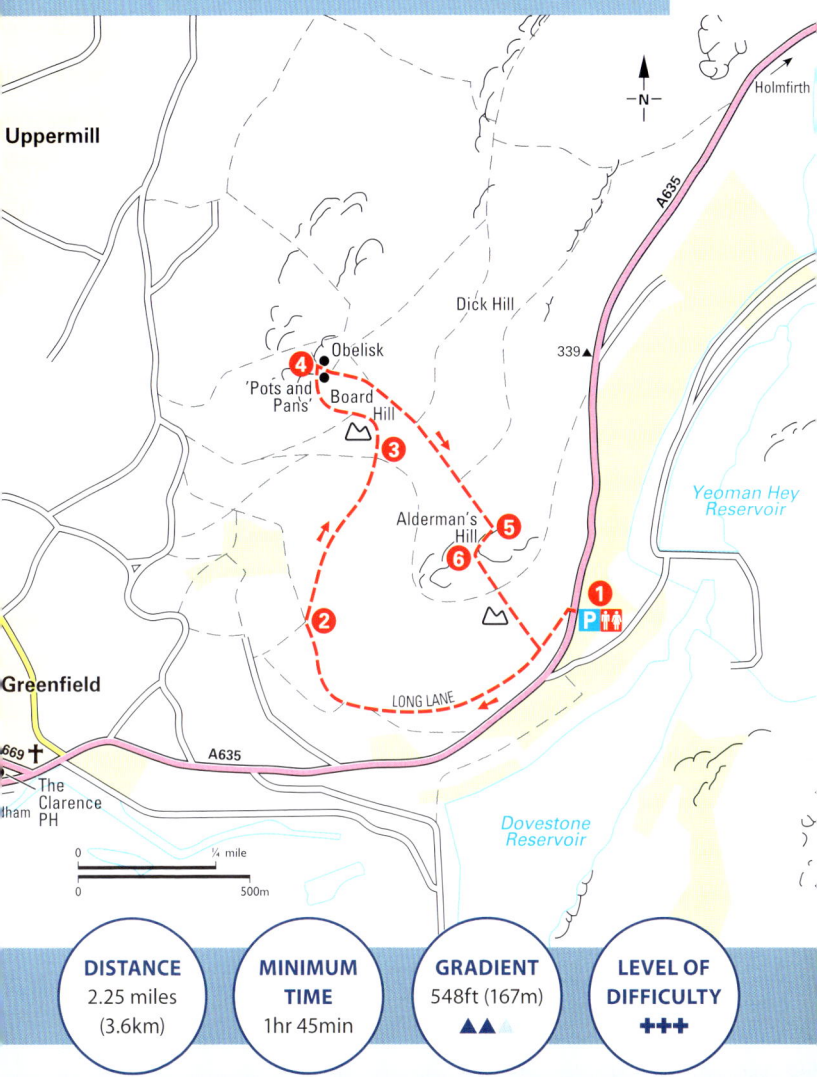

DISTANCE	MINIMUM TIME	GRADIENT	LEVEL OF DIFFICULTY
2.25 miles (3.6km)	1hr 45min	548ft (167m) ▲▲	+++

PATHS Field and moorland paths, one long and steep grassy descent which is likely to be slippery if wet **LANDSCAPE** Rugged moorland valley
SUGGESTED MAP OS Explorer OL1 Dark Peak
START/FINISH Grid reference: SE 018044
DOG FRIENDLINESS Livestock throughout, so on lead or under very close control
PARKING Binn Green pay car park
PUBLIC TOILETS At car park

Dovestone 15

Walk 2 Dovestone

WALK 2 DIRECTIONS

1 From the car park entrance cross the road and take the path through the gate opposite, waymarked 'Oldham Way'. Follow the broad and grassy track ahead which soon becomes a level walled route called Long Lane. Continue as it swings westwards around the hillside for 0.75 miles (1.2km).

2 At a junction of routes go right, over a stile by a gate, still following waymarks for the Oldham Way. Head up the obvious grassy track, aiming to the right of the hilltop obelisk. At the end of a short section enclosed by tumbledown walls you get to an old stile.

3 Go over this and out on to open moorland, following the clear path steeply uphill towards the top. Veer to the left of an old quarry and on to the memorial and rocky outcrops by the summit.

> **EATING AND DRINKING**
> The nearest place is The Clarence, a bar and restaurant that's open daily and located a mile (1.6km) west on the A635 at the mini-roundabout approaching Greenfield. If you're just after an ice cream and a cold drink there's often an ice cream van at the visitor car park by the sailing club at Dove Stone Reservoir.

4 Head south-east from the obelisk on a path parallel to the black railings, but not through a tempting gap in them. At the end of the railings follow the public footpath out across the undulating moorland, staying on the upper slopes all the way to the top of Alderman's Hill. If you want a straightforward descent return on the outward route.

5 After admiring the views of Dove Stone Reservoir from the top of the crags, turn right and walk along the high grassy edge on a clear path. Follow it down to the bottom of a slight dip.

6 The path now turns left and makes a long, steep descent of the rough but mainly grassy hillside. It joins a wall on the right and continues directly downhill towards the reservoir. At the bottom turn left on the outward route to return to the car park, or veer left above the fence on a faint path that drops down to cross a stile near the road.

> **IN THE AREA**
> For a more low level and sedate outing there's a 2.5-mile (4km) waymarked walk around tranquil Dove Stone Reservoir, away from busy roads, which you can access either from Binn Green car park or over by the larger car park at the reservoir dam. It takes in open fields, moors and woodland and is a very enjoyable short walk.

New Mills Walk 3

THE PARK UNDER THE TOWN

New Mills may be a traditional Derbyshire mill town, but the rivers below hold some surprises.

If all you see of New Mills is its central streets and shops you are missing out on something quite remarkable. The town sits above two deep gorges where the Goyt and Sett rivers converge, and despite its relative inaccessibility, early industrial mill builders soon moved in and took advantage of the fast-flowing water to power their machinery.

Heritage Centre

You begin your walk at the New Mills Heritage Centre, full of useful information and displays. From outside the centre you can look down at the spectacular sight of the River Goyt far below in its wooded gorge. Soon you're down there yourself and at one of the highlights of the walk. The Millennium Walkway is a steel-framed aerial structure attached to the massive Victorian retaining wall of the railway above. It curves around the foot of the gorge for 525ft (160m), high above the river.

The river-bank path continues below the cliffs and wooded slopes of the Torrs Riverside Park. Beyond the four-arched Union Road Bridge, a viaduct which towers 94ft (29m) above the river, is the site of the former Torr Mill, where the Goyt and Sett meet. But although the mill was destroyed by fire a century ago, the power of the rivers is being harnessed once more, this time for environmentally friendly reasons.

Archie

The Torrs Hydro project has seen the installation of a reverse Archimedes screw turbine, powered by river water channelled downwards by gravity. The giant screw, nicknamed Archie, can be seen revolving behind protective railings, so long as there's sufficient water in the river. The project is community owned and run and the electricity it generates is sold to the nearby Co-operative store. Information boards give more details about the project and there are occasional open days at weekends. Apart from the sound of water, either from the Hydro or the nearby weir, it's a peaceful place that is completely detached from the busy town above.

Walk 3 New Mills

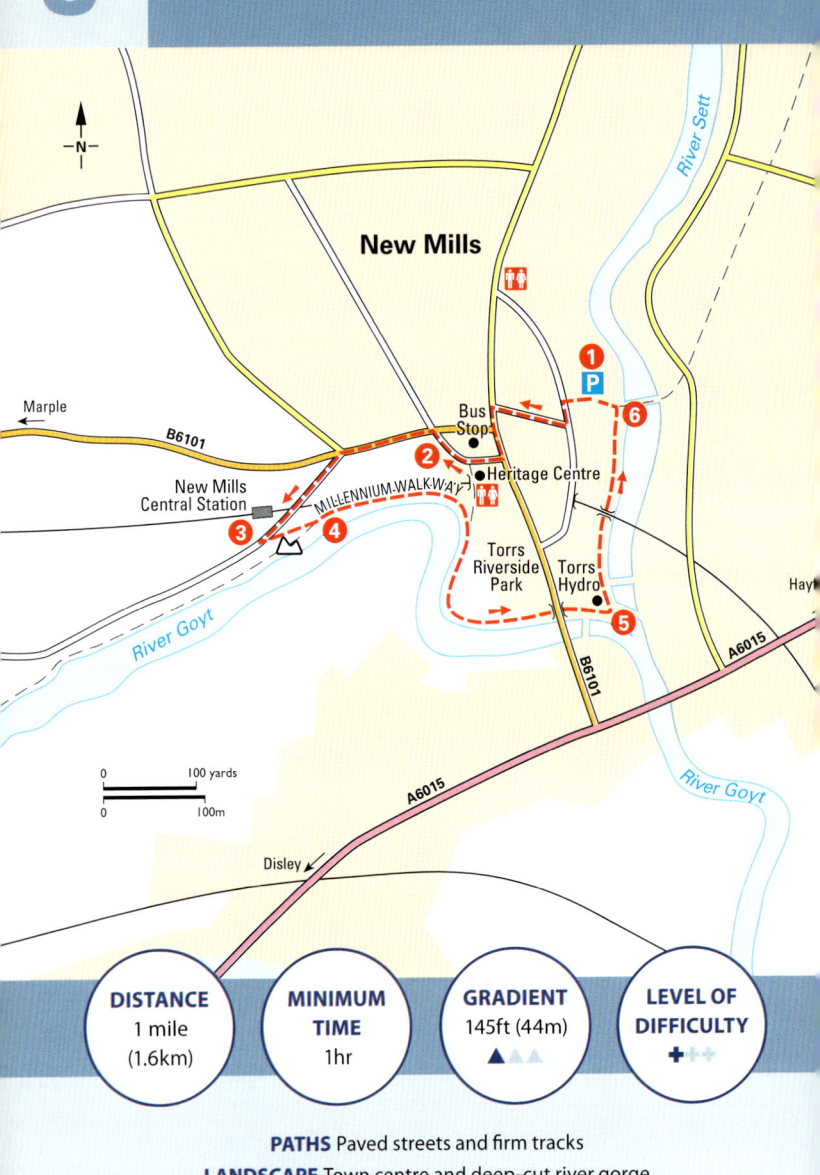

DISTANCE 1 mile (1.6km)

MINIMUM TIME 1hr

GRADIENT 145ft (44m) ▲▲▲

LEVEL OF DIFFICULTY ✚✚✚

PATHS Paved streets and firm tracks
LANDSCAPE Town centre and deep-cut river gorge
SUGGESTED MAP OS Explorer OL1 Dark Peak
START/FINISH Grid reference: SK 001854
DOG FRIENDLINESS On lead on streets, off lead by river
PARKING Torr Top pay car park
PUBLIC TOILETS Market Street and Heritage Centre

New Mills Walk 3

WALK 3 DIRECTIONS

1 From the car park entrance turn left then right, up Rock Street. At the top turn left to reach the Heritage Centre, on the far side of the roundabout below the bus stops.

2 After looking round the Heritage Centre, go out and turn right and walk up to the top of Rock Mill Lane, with views down to the River Goyt below. Turn left, then left again down Station Road to New Mills Central Station.

3 On the far side of the railway bridge turn left for a public footpath signposted 'Millennium Walkway'. Go down the steep, surfaced path and turn left at the bottom to cross the Walkway.

4 Continue on the wide and popular path beside the river through the Torrs Riverside Park. Go under a viaduct to reach the site of Torr Mill, where the Sett meets the Goyt. In front of you is the Torrs Hydro installation, with its giant Archimedes screw.

5 Now swing left, beside the River Sett, following a signpost for the Sett Valley Trail and the town centre. Don't cross the stone bridge but instead keep on the left bank. Ignore the left fork and continue beneath another viaduct.

6 At the end of the path go up some steps and turn left for more steps or a ramped path back up to the town centre. At the walled viewpoint, turn right to return to the car park.

> **EATING AND DRINKING**
>
> The Heritage Centre serves hot and cold drinks and light refreshments. Alternatively there are two cafés, Gioia Mia and Llamedos Café, both on Market Street, serving the usual range of snacks and meals.

> **IN THE AREA**
>
> Further south along the Goyt, on the edge of New Mills, is Goytside Meadows Local Nature Reserve. Threatened by a by-pass in the 1990s, these three large, flower-rich fields are now owned by the Town Council. Visitors are welcome and a leaflet guide to the 25-acre (10ha) site is available from the New Mills Heritage Centre.

> **ON THE WALK**
>
> From New Mills Central Station look back towards the town. The Midland Railway Company blasted two tunnels out of the rock face, one for the main Manchester-Sheffield line and a second for the now redundant Hayfield branch line. You will see the other side of this closed-up tunnel at the end of the walk, beyond which it has now become the Sett Valley Trail (see Walk 4).

Hayfield Walk 4

THE CHANGING FORTUNES OF HAYFIELD

Lantern Pike's lofty vantage point looks down on a village now better known for recreation rather than industry.

Hayfield once had cotton mills, papermaking mills and calico printing and dye factories. But it also had times of trouble. In 1830 it resounded to marching feet of a thousand mill workers, demanding a living wage. As was often the case in such times, the men were beaten back by soldiers and charged with civil disorder. Their industry went into a slow decline and Hayfield returned to its countryside ways.

The Sett Valley Trail
The first part of the walk follows the Sett Valley Trail, the trackbed of a railway that once linked Manchester and New Mills with Hayfield. At its peak, the steam trains would have brought thousands of people from Manchester, but since 1970 they, too, has disappeared. Today it's a pleasant tree-lined route, working its way through the valley between the hills of Lantern Pike and Chinley Churn. The track, and its former wasteland surroundings, are becoming quite a haven for wildlife. Not long after you set off, on the right, is the entrance to Bluebell Wood Local Nature Reserve.

Impressive Views
The ascent to Lantern Pike first follows a shady path through woods, then a country lane with wild flowers in the verges, and finally a path on heather and grass slopes to the rocky-crested summit. It's not one of the highest hills around, but the sense of elevation is palpable and the views back to Hayfield and Kinder Scout beyond are impressive. Lantern Pike's name comes from the beacon tower that once stood on its summit. It had to be demolished in 1907 after falling into a dangerous state of disrepair.

Mass Trespass
On the return leg you'll notice waymarks for 'Kinder Trespass 75'. This is a 14-mile (22.5km) route from New Mills devised to commemorate the 75th anniversary of the Kinder Scout Mass Trespass, when working class men and women went on to the private moors above Hayfield to demand access.

Opposite: Hayfield in the Sett Valley

Walk 4 | Hayfield

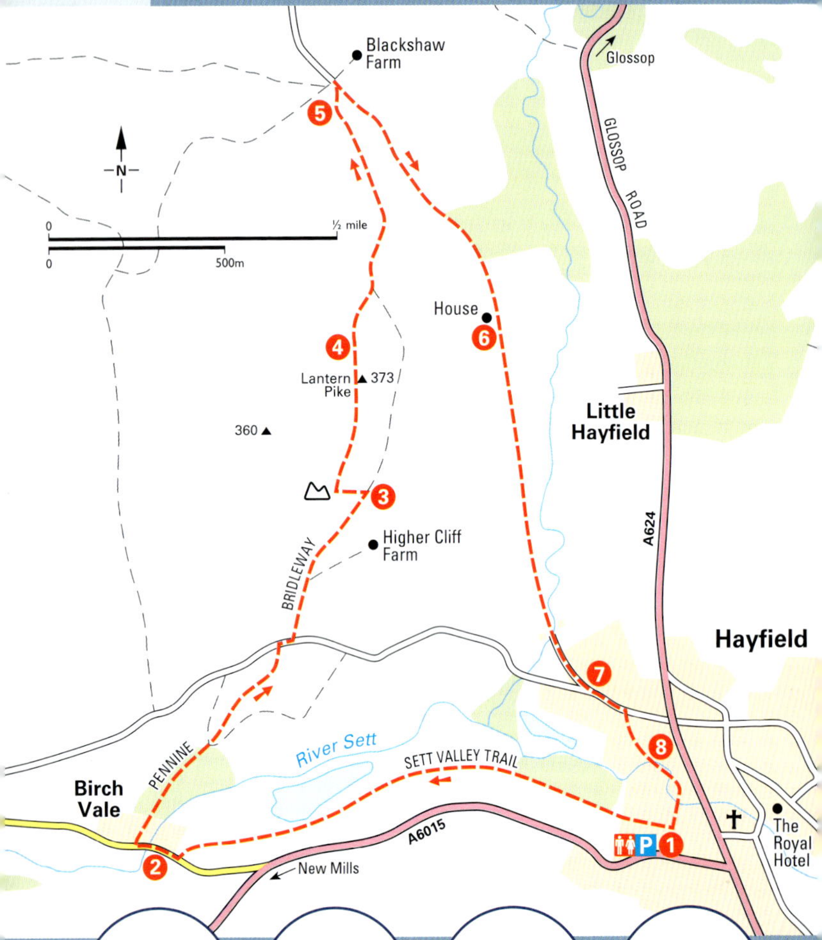

DISTANCE	MINIMUM TIME	GRADIENT	LEVEL OF DIFFICULTY
4 miles (6.4km)	2hrs 30min	665ft (202m) ▲▲▲	++

PATHS Good paths and tracks, 3 stiles
LANDSCAPE Heather moorland and rolling farm pastures
SUGGESTED MAP OS Explorer OL1 Dark Peak
START/FINISH Grid reference: SK 036869
DOG FRIENDLINESS Mostly good, but on lead in livestock fields beyond Lantern Pike **PARKING** Sett Valley Trail pay car park, Hayfield
PUBLIC TOILETS At car park

22 40 Short Walks in the Peak District

Hayfield Walk 4

WALK 4 DIRECTIONS

1 From the car park in Hayfield follow the old railway trackbed signed 'The Sett Valley Trail'. This heads west down the valley and above the River Sett to come out on a road. Turn right and walk along it for 200yds (183m).

2 Turn right up a cobbled track behind the cottages of the Crescent. Beyond a gate, the track meets a tarred farm lane at a hairpin bend. Follow the higher course to reach a road. Go right, then left beside cottages for a steep surfaced lane further up the hillside. Go straight on at the junction with Higher Cliff Farm.

3 Go through a gate, by the National Trust sign for Lantern Pike, and leave the bridleway here. Turn left along a grassy wall-side path climbing heather and bracken slopes to the rock-fringed ridge. Turn right and ascend the airy crest to Lantern Pike's summit, which is topped by a view indicator.

4 From here the path continues northwards, descending to a gate at the far boundary of the National Trust estate, where it rejoins the track you left earlier. Follow this northwards across high pastures to a five-way footpath signpost to the west of Blackshaw Farm.

5 Don't go through the gate, instead turn hard right, almost back on yourself, for the path signposted 'Hayfield via Little Hayfield'. Follow the wall on the left across the slope then down the edge of woodland. Keep going downhill on the main path until you cross a stile by a house.

> **EATING AND DRINKING**
> The Royal Hotel, beside the cricket pitch in Hayfield, is spacious and welcomes hungry walkers and families. Food is served daily in the bar and restaurant, and there's patio seating outside.

6 Ignore the second stile immediately ahead, but instead turn right and walk along the driveway, which is a public footpath, heading gently downhill. At the hairpin go straight on along a bridleway, then fork left for a path down to cottages. Cross the river and beyond the buildings walk out along the road to enter Hayfield.

7 At the junction at the end turn left and walk along the pavement. Just before the overhead bridge go right, by a notice board about the Calico Trail, and out across an open patch of ground known as the Old School Field. Follow the path to the far left corner.

8 Go right over the footbridge among the trees, then follow the path along the bank of the River Sett and up between new houses. Turn left to return to the car park. The village centre is to the left, across the A624 (pedestrian crossing or underpass).

Walk 5: Woodlands Valley

THE SNAKE'S WOODLAND RETREAT

A gentle wander through the woods of a remote valley beside a famous moorland road.

This short and relatively easy forest walk explores Woodlands Valley, which carries the A57 Manchester–Sheffield road up and over the notorious Snake Pass. The Snake Pass crosses the inhospitable moorland between Kinder Scout and Bleaklow, reaching 1,679ft (512m) at its summit and gets the worst of the British weather, which often forces the road to close in winter.

Snake Pass

Because of its combination of tight bends and straights, the Snake Pass is popular with motorcyclists, but its length and average gradient (about 1 in 7 for over 3 miles (4.8km) on the western side) also makes it one of only a handful of UK road climbs that are comparable to continental road cycling, so it features on many domestic road races.

Apart from a few scattered farms and the Snake Pass Inn, built originally as a staging post for weary travellers, the valley is mostly given over to farming and forestry. Once you cross the road from the Birchin Clough Bridge lay-by and descend into the conifer plantations, tucked below Lady Clough Moor, you soon lose the sight and sound of the traffic. Indeed, the trees provide welcome shelter from the elements, even if it's blowing hard on the open moors above.

Ashop Clough

The route makes its way gently across the hillside before dropping down to meet a public footpath at the foot of Ashop Clough. This is the walkers' equivalent of the Snake Pass, a long and taxing west–east route from Hayfield that climbs up the side of Mill Hill on the edge of Kinder Scout and heads down Black Ashop Moor to reach the Woodlands Valley.

You follow this footpath for just a short distance, before heading back up the main valley on a waterside track into the heart of the woods. If you want to extend the route you can continue northwards on waymarked paths further up Lady Clough, but towards the open moor the paths become steeper and muddier.

Woodlands Valley

Walk 5

DISTANCE	MINIMUM TIME	GRADIENT	LEVEL OF DIFFICULTY
1.25 miles (2km)	1hr	278ft (85m) ▲	✚

PATHS Woodland tracks and paths, sometimes a little boggy by the river
LANDSCAPE Narrow, wooded valley, surrounded by high moorland
SUGGESTED MAP OS Explorer OL1 Dark Peak
START/FINISH Grid reference: SK 109914
DOG FRIENDLINESS Good off-lead route
PARKING Birchin Clough Bridge lay-by on A57
PUBLIC TOILETS None on route

Woodlands Valley 25

Walk 5: Woodlands Valley

WALK 5 DIRECTIONS

1 From the lay-by cross the road carefully and beside the forest sign descend the paved, zig-zag path into the wooded valley. Go through a gate and on through the pines next to a stream until you reach a footbridge.

2 Cross the bridge and continue along the path down the valley, with the water on your right, until you reach the sweeping, open bend of a forest road by a vehicle bridge.

3 Turn right, across the bridge, and follow the forest road as it makes its way gradually uphill. Keep straight on at a junction, rising higher above the valley floor, until the track begins to bend to the right.

4 Turn left, following white waymarked posts for a narrow path downhill that swings right and continues descending. At the bottom, go down a few steps to reach the junction with a public footpath.

5 Turn left and beyond a stile emerge from the trees and follow the rocky path alongside the River Ashop, with the plantation on your left. Follow this route along the bottom of Ashop Clough until you reach a long wooden footbridge.

6 Cross the bridge and at the path junction on the far side go ahead through the gate and back into the woodland. This path stays close to the river and eventually reaches the junction with the forest road at Point **3**. Go straight over for the path back up to the start.

> **ON THE WALK**
> Although conifer plantations are not as rich in wildlife as broadleaved woods, small birds like the tit family are quite plentiful. Blue, great and coal tits are all to be found in the woods, flitting among the branches where they feed on insects and seeds.

> **EATING AND DRINKING**
> The Snake Pass Inn is located less than a mile (1.6km) south on the A57 and is the obvious place to stop for refreshment. It offers a wide range of bar meals, as well as lighter snacks and hot beverages.

> **IN THE AREA**
> It's worth driving the short distance up to the summit of the Snake Pass to sample both its wild habitat and also the sheer remoteness of the location. You can pull in at the very top, the point at which Pennine Way walkers cross the road on their lonely passage across Kinder Scout and Bleaklow. It's not for the faint-hearted.

Edale Walk 6

KINDER SCOUT'S MOORLAND MAJESTY

An energetic ascent of the high moors above Edale gives a real flavour of the Dark Peak.

Edale sits peacefully amid pasture, riverside meadow and hedgerow, surrounded by a high moorland backdrop. The hills of the Mam Tor ridge lie across the valley to the south, but immediately to the north are the crags of Kinder Scout. Strictly speaking Edale consists of five scattered hamlets or booths, but nowadays the main village is centred on Grindsbrook Booth that you walk through as you set off for Kinder Scout. On the edge of the village is the Old Nags Head pub, the starting place for the Pennine Way National Trail.

Rambling Man

In depression torn 1930s England, Tom Stephenson, then secretary of the Ramblers' Association, told the readers of the *Daily Herald* of his dream to create a 'long, green trail' across the roof of England. This dream would bring Edale to the world's attention. It took 30 years, endless campaigning and Acts of Parliament to achieve, but in 1965 the Pennine Way was opened. Spanning 268 miles (431km) from Edale to Kirk Yetholm in Scotland, it was Britain's first official long distance footpath and is arguably still the most challenging in terms of height and terrain.

Ringing Roger

Originally the Pennine Way headed up beside Grinds Brook, then it crossed the middle of the Kinder Scout plateau, but the inhospitable peat bogs made for a stiff navigational challenge, especially as this was only day one! Following escalating erosion the route was switched to Jacob's Ladder, further up the valley. On this walk you can step out on the first few yards of the original route, before a long but straightforward climb up to Ringing Roger, the so-called echoing rocks. The views up and down the Edale valley and across to the Lose Hill–Mam Tor ridge are superb. Ringing Roger is just one of a number of weirdly shaped gritstone outcrops that dot the summit plateau of Kinder Scout. They're matched only by the oddness of their names, with others including Seal Stones, Boxing Glove Stones, Wool Packs and Madwoman's Stones.

Walk 6 Edale

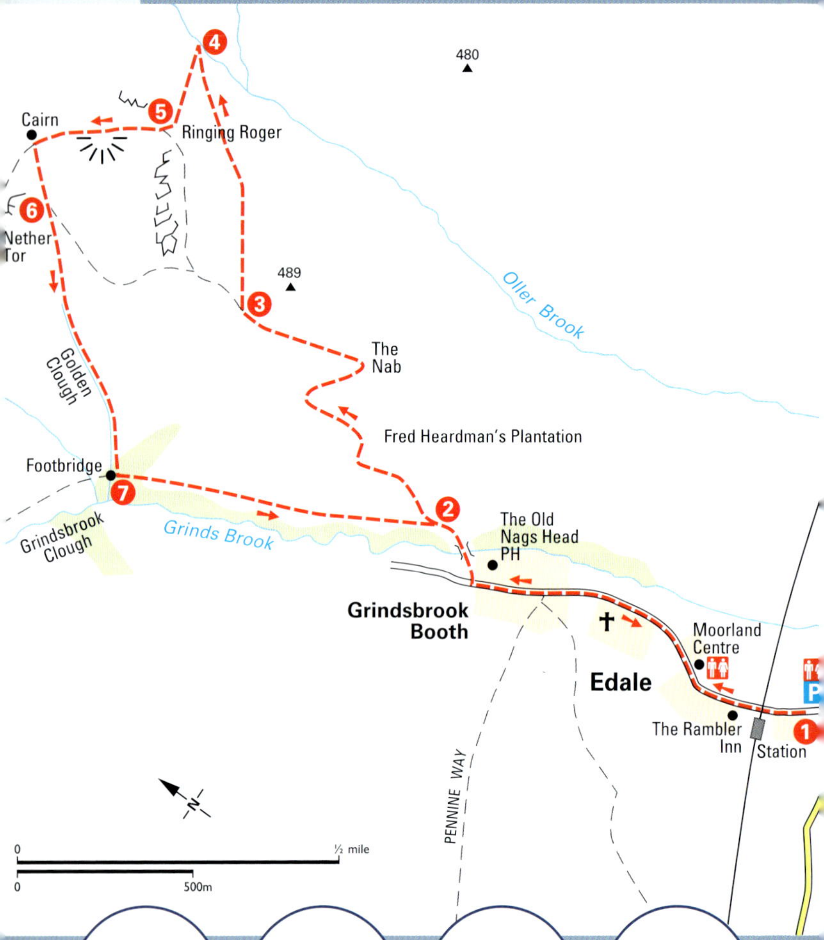

DISTANCE
3.75 miles (6km)

MINIMUM TIME
3hrs

GRADIENT
1,066ft (325m)
▲▲▲

LEVEL OF DIFFICULTY
+++

PATHS Rock and peat paths, some steep and rough
LANDSCAPE Heather moor and steep cloughs (valleys)
SUGGESTED MAP OS Explorer OL1 Dark Peak
START/FINISH Grid reference: SK 123853
DOG FRIENDLINESS This is sheep country, so dogs on lead
PARKING Edale pay car park
PUBLIC TOILETS At car park and Moorland Centre

28   40 Short Walks in the Peak District

Edale Walk 6

WALK 6 DIRECTIONS

1 Turn right out of the car park, beside the toilet block, and head north along the lane, under the railway and past the Moorland Centre and Old Nags Head. At the very far end, by white gates, turn right and follow the path down to cross Grinds Brook by a footbridge. Go up the other side on the main path.

2 Leave the main Grindsbrook Clough path alongside the side of a barn, taking the right fork that climbs up the lower slope to a gate on the edge of open country. Beyond the stile the path zig-zags above Fred Heardman's Plantation then climbs up the nose of The Nab towards the skyline rocks.

3 Below the final, eroded section up to the summit there's a dip. Just before this dip fork right for a long, slanting path to the right of Ringing Roger. Follow this all the way up to the top.

4 When you reach the top head left and follow the path along the edge all the way to the weirdly shaped rocks of Ringing Roger.

EATING AND DRINKING

The Old Nags Head and The Rambler Inn at Edale both serve bar meals, and there's equally good café refreshment at Cooper's Café by Edale Post Office and at the National Trust's Penny Pot Café by the railway station.

5 After inspecting the rocks swing north on a level path to the top of Golden Clough. At a huge cairn turn sharply left for a clear path downhill.

6 After 100yds (91m) fork right on a fainter path down through the bracken above the stream in the bottom of the clough. Further down it steepens and follows the stream itself. For a more straightforward descent stay on the main path that swings around to meet the outward route below Ringing Roger near Point **3**.

7 The path emerges at the bottom of Golden Clough by an arched wooden footbridge which carries the original Pennine Way up Grindsbrook Clough. Don't cross it but instead turn left, go through the gate for a short woodland path, then a paved route back to Edale.

ON THE WALK

Near the start of the walk you pass the Moorland Centre, opened in 2006 by the Peak District National Park as an information and research centre about the unique natural habitat which makes up most of the Dark Peak. It's also a good place to buy maps and check the latest weather forecast.

Win Hill Walk 7

WINNING VIEWS FROM A REAL PEAK

Scale the shapely summit of Win Hill, one of the Peak District's mini mountains.

It's an irony of the Peak District that few of its hills have any real angled peaks, like the mountains of the Lake District, but Win Hill is certainly one of them. It might be only a pointed pimple at the end of a moorland ridge, but the coned summit gives it that elevation that catches the eye from below – and offers 360-degree views once you've puffed your way up to the top.

Ladybower Reservoir

There's a sedate beginning to the walk on the shores of Ladybower Reservoir. When the reservoir is full, it holds back 6.1 billion gallons (27,730 megalitres) of water. Interpretation boards explain some of the peculiar features of this impressive construction, including draw-off towers and bellmouth spillway shafts. There's also information on the work undertaken in 1998–9 to refurbish Ladybower Dam, which involved quarrying stone from the forested hillside below Win Hill. You can still see the area, since relandscaped and replanted, where the rock was extracted.

Rocky Ridge

Soon you enter the wooded hillside, heading upwards for the moors and the rocky summit ridge of Win Hill. From the 1,515ft (462m) top the views encompass the broad Dark Peak sweep of Kinder Scout, Bleaklow and the Derwent Moors, with the valleys of woodland and water reaching deep into the upland massif. Over the moors to the east lies Sheffield, while immediately to the south-east are the communities of Bamford and Hathersage, with the Derwent Valley extending into the distance. West lies the Hope Valley, with Castleton and Mam Tor prominent at its head, while no less mistakable is the tall chimney of the Hope cement works.

The nearest hill to the west is Lose Hill, on the far side of the River Noe. According to local legend, the valley was the site of a Dark Ages battle when King Edwin of Northumbria beat King Cuicholm of Wessex after a failed assassination attempt. Cuicholm's defeated army camped on Lose Hill, while Edwin and the victors occupied – of course – Win Hill.

Opposite: Panorama over Ladybower Reservoir

Walk 7: Win Hill

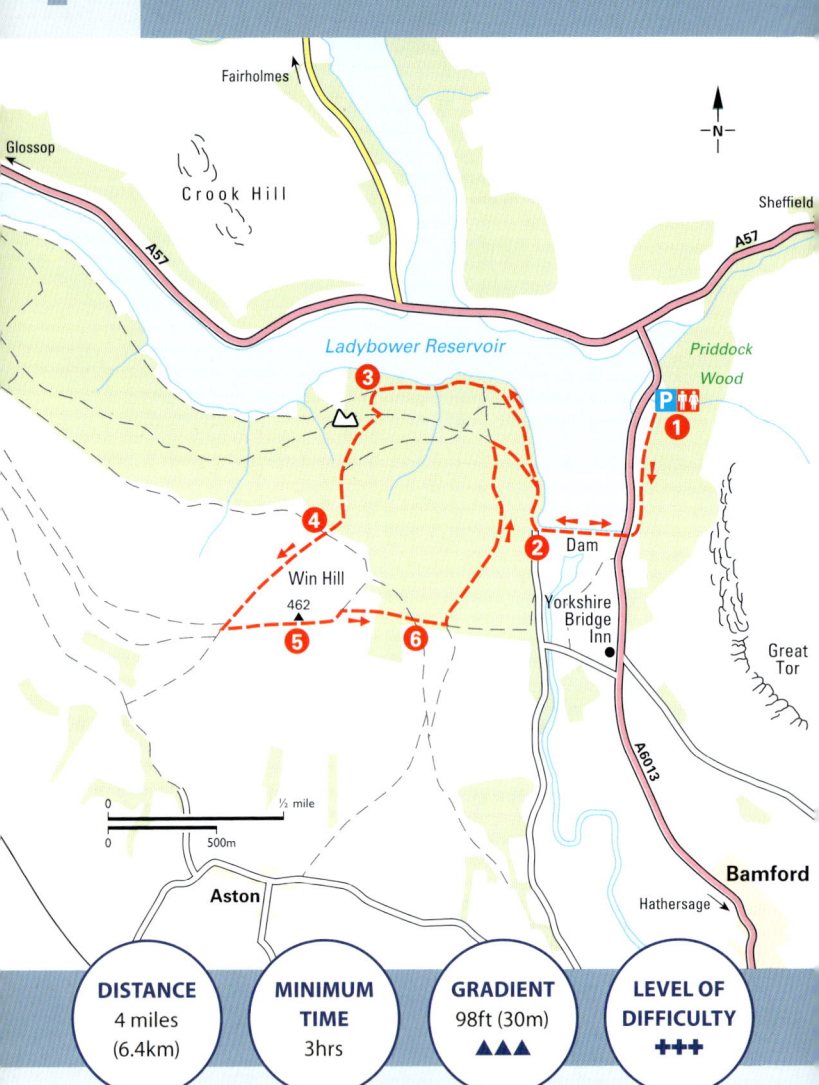

DISTANCE
4 miles (6.4km)

MINIMUM TIME
3hrs

GRADIENT
98ft (30m) ▲▲▲

LEVEL OF DIFFICULTY
+++

PATHS Hard tracks, moorland and woodland paths, sometimes muddy
LANDSCAPE Flooded valley surrounded by woodland and open moors
SUGGESTED MAP OS Explorer OL1 Dark Peak
START/FINISH Grid reference: SK 202859
DOG FRIENDLINESS Off lead on enclosed tracks and in woodland, but on lead around sheep on moors
PARKING Heatherdene pay car park **PUBLIC TOILETS** At car park

Win Hill Walk 7

WALK 7 DIRECTIONS

1 From the far southern end of the car park walk along the surfaced path past the toilets and picnic shelter towards Ladybower Dam. Follow it down to cross the road by the memorial stone, then walk over the dam to the far side.

2 Turn right and follow the broad track above the curving shore for just under one mile (1.6km). As you approach a clearing look for a signpost on the left, indicated 'Win Hill'.

3 Turn left for an initially steep path that crosses another path and continues more gently up the wooded hillside. Cross one more track, then go through a young plantation to reach the open moor.

4 At a junction of paths go ahead right for a narrow path up across the heather aiming to the right of the summit. At the ridge at the top turn left for the path to the very top.

5 Carry on past the summit and head east down a stone pitched path, across open slopes, and into woodland. At a crossroads of tracks go through the gate ahead, signed 'Yorkshire Bridge'.

6 In a few paces fork left and at the bottom of this short path turn left on to a broad, gentle track through the plantation. After 0.5 miles (800m) turn sharply right through a small wooden gate for a public footpath down to the shoreline track. Turn right to reach the dam and return to the start.

EATING AND DRINKING
The Yorkshire Bridge Inn, just along from Ladybower dam, is popular with visitors and serves bar meals every lunchtime and evening. For freshly made rolls, snacks and savouries head for the Bamford Bakery in the centre of the village, another mile (1.6km) along the road.

IN THE AREA
To find out more about the history of the Upper Derwent reservoirs, including the drowned villages that made way for them and the temporary community that grew up during their construction, head north to the visitor centre at Fairholmes (off the A57). You can also learn how the famous Dambusters of 617 Squadron trained here before their raids on German dams in the Second World War.

ON THE WALK
Near the dam you might see a waymark for the Touchstone Trail. This was created by the local community of Bamford to celebrate the Millennium and consists of a 5-mile (8km) walking route around the village visiting sculptures or 'touchstones' representing earth, water, fire and air. A leaflet guide is available from Bamford post office.

Walk 8: Rivelin & Redmires

FROM BABBLING BROOK TO MOORLAND HEIGHTS

The wooded Rivelin Valley and the heather moors above Redmires make for a wildlife walk of contrasts.

This is a walk all about the contrasting wildlife habitats you can encounter in just one short walk in the Peak District. It begins with an exploration of Wyming Brook Nature Reserve, managed by Sheffield Wildlife Trust. The route follows the gurgling brook as it makes its way down a deep, often rocky valley, much of it shaded by trees. Dippers perch on boulders amid the fast-running water; while the surrounding woodland floor is renowned for its display of fungi in the autumn.

Woodland and Moorland Birds

On entering the main Rivelin Valley you swing westwards above the reservoir through a tremendous mix of trees – beech, sweet chestnut, oak, birch and Scots pine are all present. Such a rich variety of trees inevitably supports a wide range of woodland birds, including goldcrests and even crossbills.

The second half of the walk is completely different, taking you out of the valley woodland and on to the open moors. Instead of pheasants skulking about in the undergrowth, you'll see red grouse. The moorland is also the place to see the merlin, which is smaller, faster and more agile than a kestrel.

Sheffield Wildlife Trust

An easy path alongside a conduit or water channel gives great views back across Rivelin Valley and over to distant Sheffield. Closer to hand is Hammond's Field, reached by a short access path as you approach Redmires Reservoir. A traditional piece of in-bye farmland (enclosed fields below the open moors, close to farm dwellings), Sheffield Wildlife Trust has left it in its natural state, a rough and boggy patch of ground that supports curlew and snipe, newts and toads, as well as a whole host of grasses and plants – Yorkshire fog, marsh foxtail and cuckooflower to name but three.

The walk ends near Redmires Reservoir which, if you want to extend the route, can be explored more fully. Despite its seemingly bleak appearance, over 160 different species of bird have been recorded here, and because of its height and location it's particularly well-used by migrating geese.

Rivelin & Redmires

Walk 8

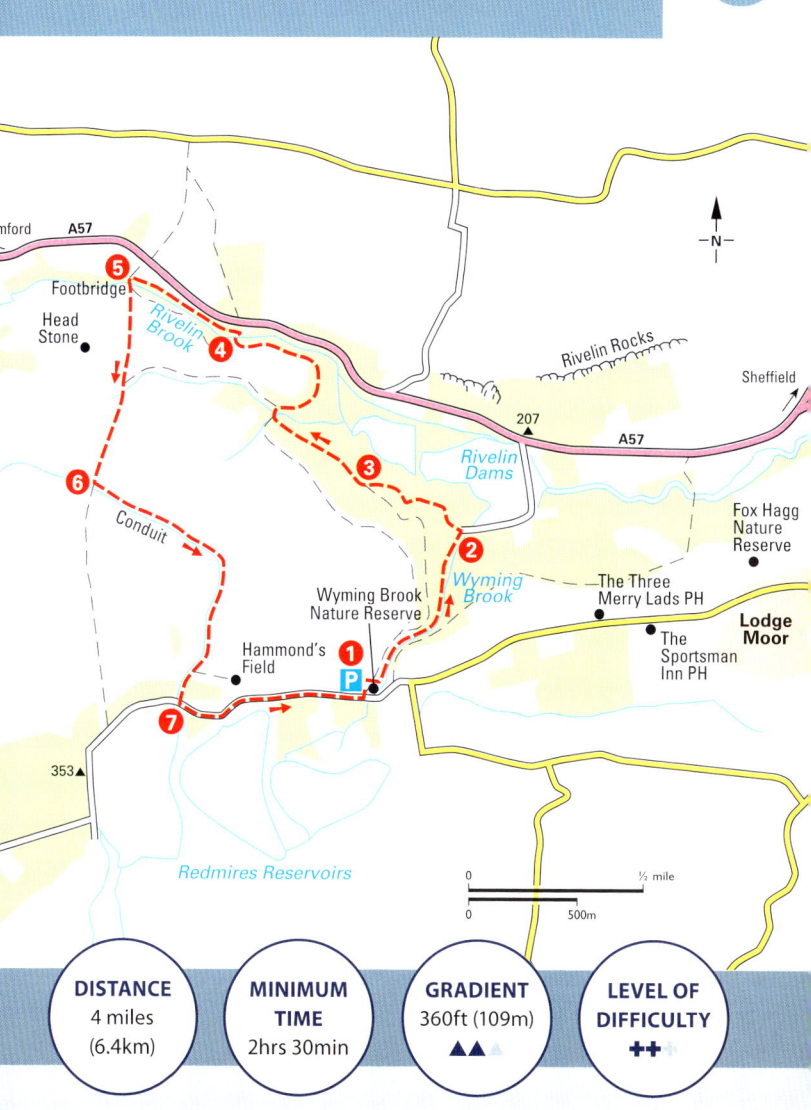

DISTANCE 4 miles (6.4km)

MINIMUM TIME 2hrs 30min

GRADIENT 360ft (109m) ▲▲

LEVEL OF DIFFICULTY ++

PATHS Woodland paths, some rocky and occasionally muddy, sandy moorland tracks, road, 1 stile
LANDSCAPE Deep wooded valley and open heather moors
SUGGESTED MAP OS Explorer OL1 Dark Peak
START/FINISH Grid reference: SK 271858
DOG FRIENDLINESS Fine in woods, but on lead on moorland section
PARKING Wyming Brook car park **PUBLIC TOILETS** None on route

Rivelin & Redmires 35

Walk 8: Rivelin & Redmires

WALK 8 DIRECTIONS

1 At the far end of the car park take the right-hand path and go down to cross the brook by stepping stones. Fork left and follow the sometimes rocky path beside the brook along the foot of the deepening, wooded valley. Continue steadily downstream, crossing and re-crossing by a succession of footbridges.

2 At the bottom of the valley go down some steps and through a metal gate on to a wide track. Ahead there's a small clearing and glimpses of Rivelin Reservoir through the trees. Turn left and follow the broad, gently rising track as it curves its way through woodland.

3 At a wide junction by an embankment wall go, straight on still amid the trees. Gradually drop downhill until you reach a stone bridge over Rivelin Brook.

4 Cross the bridge and go left on to the signposted public footpath on the far bank. Go over some rocks then down to the narrow path beside the tree-lined brook. When you come to a footbridge, turn left to cross it.

> **ON THE WALK**
>
> As you make your way up across the moorland from the Rivelin Valley, there's a curious feature over to your right. The Head Stone is an oddly shaped gritstone outcrop that sits high and proud on its own amid the heather. Take a short detour and decide for yourself what it resembles.

5 Follow the path up on to open moorland. Go through a kissing gate and continue on the path directly up the heather-clad hillside, keeping straight on at a junction. Cross a stile, the only one of the walk, then immediately turn left.

6 Now follow the level embankment of a conduit or water channel, as it curves around the open hilltop, passing some handily placed benches. Continue all the way along until you reach Redmires Road, opposite the dam of the top reservoir.

7 Turn left and follow the road back down to the entrance to Wyming Brook Nature Reserve and the car park. If you have more time, you might want to explore nearby Fox Hagg Nature Reserve, to the east of Wyming Brook.

> **EATING AND DRINKING**
>
> The two pubs just back along Redmires Road both serve food at lunchtime and in the evenings and are worth visiting. The Three Merry Lads has outdoor seating and a children's play area that overlooks the Rivelin Valley, while at The Sportsman Inn you can enjoy a pint while watching the cricket on the playing fields by the pub.

Lyme Park
Walk 9

A CLASSIC ESTATE WALK

A circuit of the attractive grounds of Lyme Park, one of the Peak's finest country houses.

It's the classic English stately home: a medieval manor house that was gradually transformed into a large and elegant Palladian mansion, and which is today full of antique furniture and tapestries, carvings and clocks. Outside, there are formal gardens (including an Edwardian Rose Garden and an Orangery), plus 1,400 acres (567ha) of gorgeous open moorland and parkland that is home to herds of red and fallow deer.

Lyme Park was originally created by Richard II who, in 1398, granted land in the Royal Forest of Macclesfield. It became the ancestral home of the Legh family for the next five and a half centuries, and they were responsible for developing the original house into the sumptuous pile that you see today. In 1946 the entire estate was donated to the National Trust. The grounds are open all year and the lovely rolling parkland and moorland tracks with their fabulous views are well worth exploring.

Landmarks

This short walk visits two of the more unusual features in the Park. The Lantern is a small coned tower high up on a wooded hillside, but a gap in the trees was deliberately left so that it remained visible. These so-called vista lines were carefully plotted so that the house could be admired from surrounding locations. Another impressive corridor is through the trees of Knightslow Wood to the south of the house.

The best is kept till last, however. The curious hilltop folly known as The Cage is one of Lyme Park's most visible landmarks. An elegant three-storey building, it was built around 1735 as a banqueting house, but since then has been used as an observation tower, as a lodging for the park's gamekeepers, and even as a temporary prison for poachers. After falling derelict it was restored and is occasionally open to the public. The Cage sits high on an open ridge and offers superlative views not just across the park but also towards the Dark Peak moors, most notably to Kinder Scout. If you have taken a picnic or refreshments with you the smooth, grassy slopes below The Cage are the perfect place to linger awhile.

Walk 9 Lyme Park

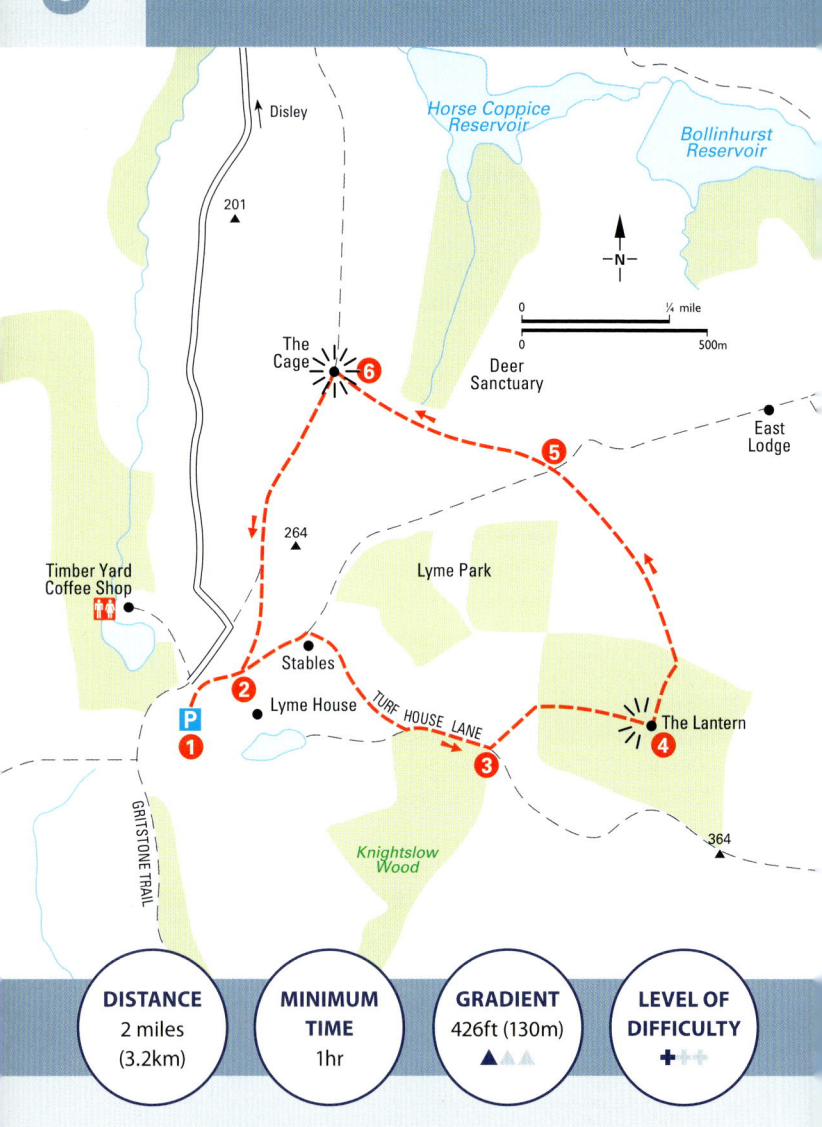

DISTANCE	MINIMUM TIME	GRADIENT	LEVEL OF DIFFICULTY
2 miles (3.2km)	1hr	426ft (130m) ▲▲▲	✚✚✚

PATHS Firm tracks and grassy paths, 3 stiles including one high ladder stile
LANDSCAPE Rolling parkland and fields edging the moors
SUGGESTED MAP OS Explorer OL1 Dark Peak
START/FINISH Grid reference: SJ 964823
DOG FRIENDLINESS On lead around livestock, otherwise under control
PARKING Lyme Park, off A6 (free to National Trust members)
PUBLIC TOILETS By Timber Yard Coffee Shop, near main car park

Lyme Park Walk 9

WALK 9 DIRECTIONS

❶ From the car park go up the stepped path next to the information centre and refreshment kiosk to reach the imposing front entrance to Lyme House.

❷ Join the main driveway as it does an 'S' bend uphill. Fork left in front of the Stables then immediately afterwards turn right on a smaller track between stone gateposts. Go through a gate and continue along this route out into the park, alongside a plantation.

> **ON THE WALK**
>
> The track from behind the Stables leading towards The Lantern is known as Turf House Lane. This unusual name was taken from the turf-built shelters that were once constructed alongside the lane for use as outdoor larders in which to store food.

❸ When you reach a gate and ladder stile, with the moors beyond, turn half left before them and walk up across the rough pasture to a stile in the fence. Go over this and then up a short, steep section of open hillside between the trees to reach The Lantern.

❹ Turn left and follow a woodland path until you come to a high, deer-proof wall. Cross it via a ladder stile and now follow the obvious path down the open hillside beyond, heading

> **IN THE AREA**
>
> The nearby Macclesfield Canal forms part of the Cheshire Ring Canal Walk, a 97-mile (156km) circular route around Greater Manchester incorporating the tow paths of six historic canals, including the Peak Forest and the Trent & Mersey. The stretch past Lyme Park, between Macclesfield and Marple, is rural and peaceful.

roughly in the direction of The Cage that is now visible on the distant hilltop. Cross a stile in a fence to reach a hard cross track.

❺ Go straight over and continue on the clear grassy route, with the Deer Sanctuary (no public access) to your right. Dip down to cross a small stream then climb up the far side to finally reach The Cage.

❻ Turn left and follow the top of the open ridge southwards until Lyme House appears below. Go down the easy grassy bank to return to the stepped path and back to the start.

> **EATING AND DRINKING**
>
> The Ale Cellar Restaurant inside Lyme House includes a children's menu, while the Coffee Shop at the Timber Yard, located near the car park by the large millpond and open daily in season, operates on a self-service basis and has a decent range of snacks and light refreshments.

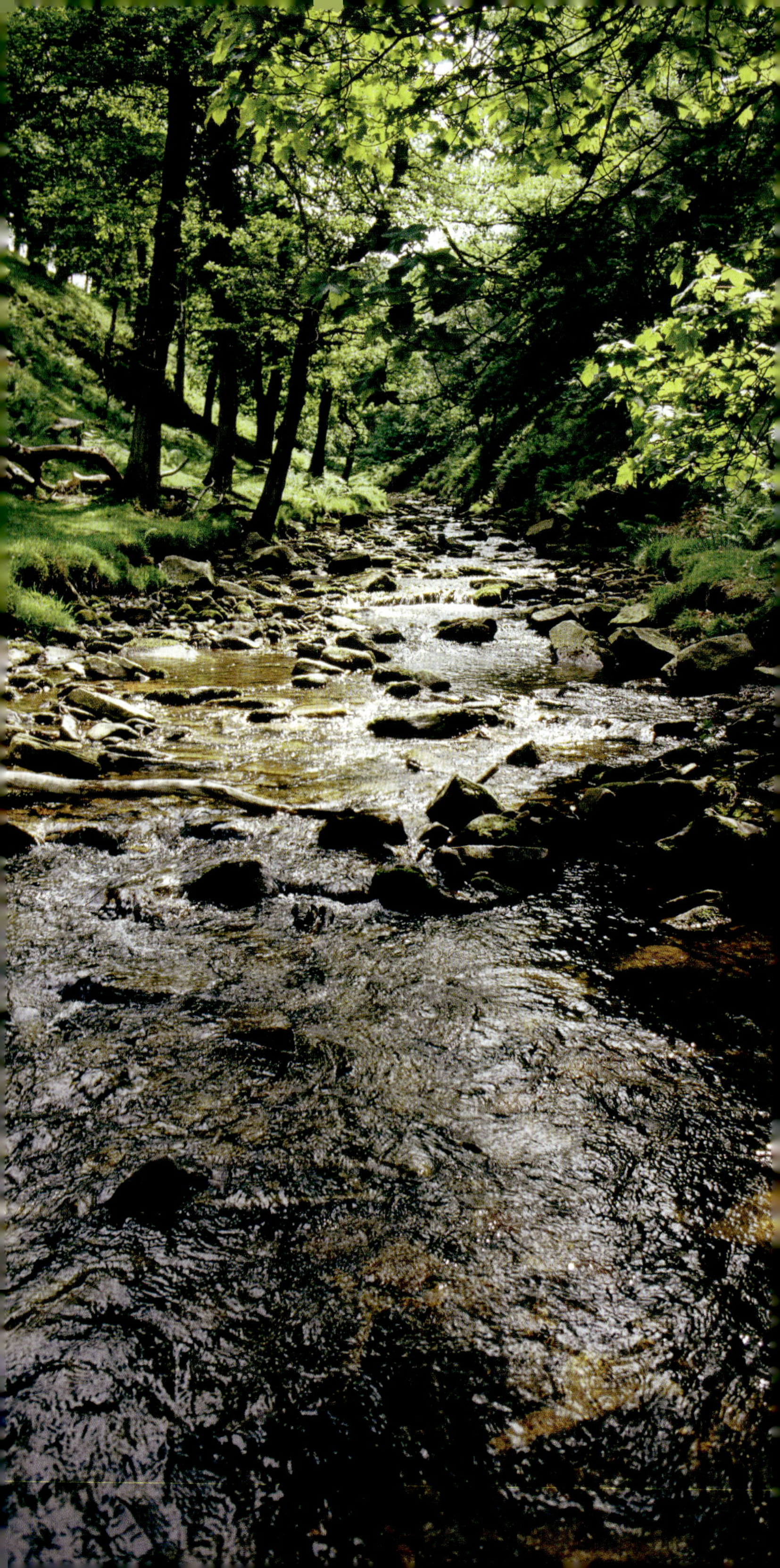

Taxal & Fernilee Reservoir

Walk 10

THE DIFFERENT FACES OF THE GOYT

Human influences have had a dramatic effect on the Goyt Valley, as this walk of two halves shows.

As befits an area of mostly high ground in the centre of England, the rivers of the Peak District drain in many different directions. The Derwent and Dove flow south to join the Trent, en route to the Humber and the North Sea; the River Rivelin heads eastwards to feed the River Don via Sheffield; while the Dane makes its way through Cheshire to the River Weaver. The principal river in the north west is the Goyt, flowing initially northwards via Whaley Bridge and New Mills, where it's joined by the Sett, then on to on to Stockport to meet the Tame and Etherow to become the River Mersey.

Gentle Valley

The Goyt rises on the high moors of Axe Edge, near the Cat and Fiddle Inn south-west of Buxton, but its narrow upper section has been transformed by the building of two reservoirs, Errwood and Fernilee (see Walk 24) and the planting of dense conifer woodlands on the western slopes. It gives the valley a harsher, perhaps rather artificial feel, but still with a sense of upland remoteness and element of wildness. This walk, on the other hand, covers the area below the reservoirs and presents a broader and gentler valley of more mixed habitat, including wooded lower slopes and enclosed farmland.

It's also a walk of two halves, both giving a different perspective of the valley. The route up to Fernilee Reservoir is along the valley floor, initially on paths through woodland of oak, birch and beech. Soon you are out into riverside meadows, following the river bank, before climbing up past waterworks buildings to cross the dam.

Taxal

The route back follows farm tracks high on the western slopes of the valley, giving sweeping views across the Goyt to the distant moors. As you wander down to the hamlet of Taxal, broadleaved woodland clothes the valley floor, above which is walled pasture and a few ploughed fields, then managed moorland higher up. It's a reminder, despite National Park designation, of just how much the Peak District landscape has been fashioned by human hands.

Opposite: View downstream of the River Goyt

Walk 10: Taxal & Fernilee Reservoir

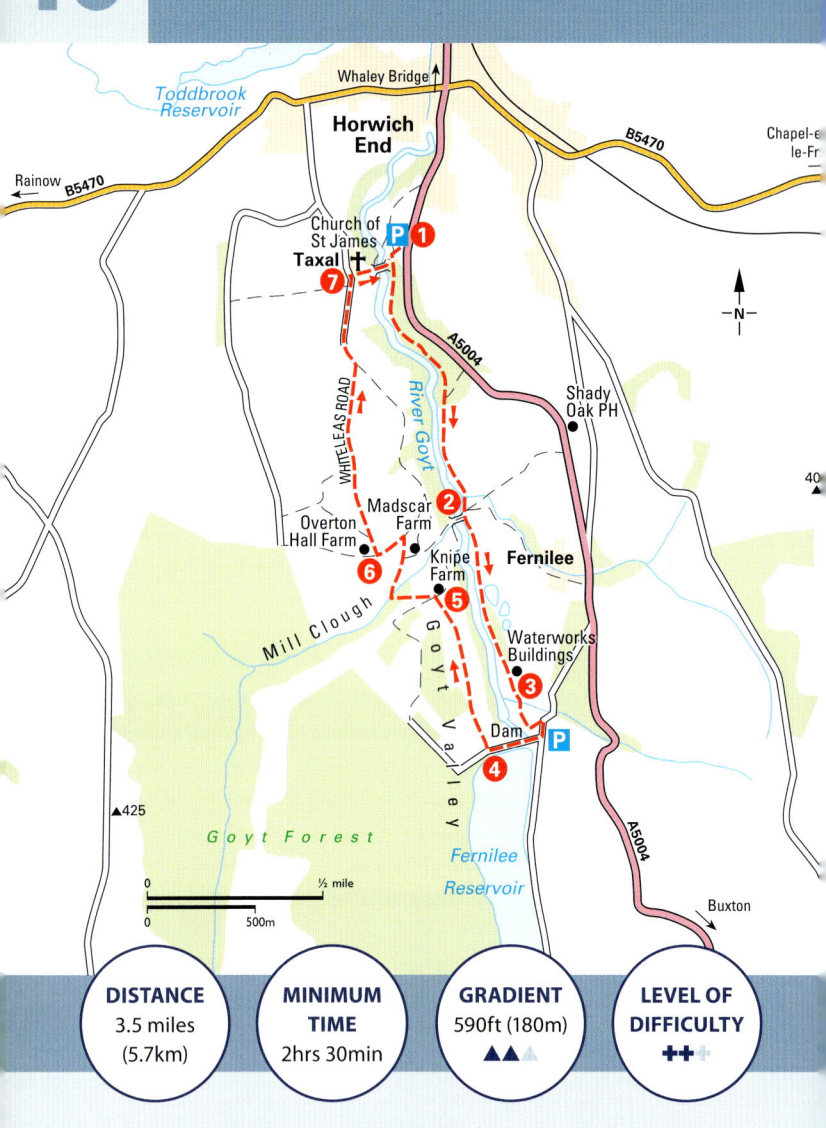

DISTANCE 3.5 miles (5.7km)

MINIMUM TIME 2hrs 30min

GRADIENT 590ft (180m) ▲▲

LEVEL OF DIFFICULTY ++

PATHS Unmade lanes, grass and woodland paths, sometimes muddy
LANDSCAPE Wide river valley with woodland and pasture
SUGGESTED MAP OS Explorer OL24 White Peak
START/FINISH Grid reference: SK 008799
DOG FRIENDLINESS Off lead on fenced tracks, but on lead around livestock
PARKING Lay-by on A5004 south of Whaley Bridge
PUBLIC TOILETS Nearest at Whaley Bridge

42 40 Short Walks in the Peak District

Taxal & Fernilee Reservoir

Walk 10

WALK 10 DIRECTIONS

❶ From the lay-by follow the track steeply downhill. Nearing but not at the bottom go round a sharp bend and take the gated footpath on the left. Follow this route through the woods with the River Goyt below on your right. Continue across a series of wide, gated meadows, now close to the river bank, until you reach a footbridge.

❷ Ignore the bridge and stay on the east bank, carrying on across the open fields. Beyond a gate join a firmer track, and continuing in the same direction go past some woodland until eventually you reach a cluster of large and unlovely waterworks buildings.

❸ Go left, across the yard, and follow the public footpath up the tarmac drive to the very top. Turn right along the road to reach the small car park by the dam. Here turn right and go along the road across the top of Fernilee Reservoir dam to the far side.

❹ At the junction of routes turn right for a broad, stony track back along the

> ### 🍴 EATING AND DRINKING
> There are plenty of cafés and food outlets in Whaley Bridge, but for the nearest pub try the Shady Oak at Fernilee, just along the main road from the start. It's a long-time walkers' favourite, serving food lunchtime and evenings and open all day at weekends.

> ### 🔵 IN THE AREA
> While on the theme of water, visit Bugsworth Basin, just to the east of Whaley Bridge, once a busy inland port on the Peak Forest Canal which has recently been restored. There's a handy canal-themed pub on the water's edge.

valley, but this time high up on the open western slopes. Continue along this obvious route, ignoring all turnings off, until you reach Knipe Farm.

❺ Stay on the main track as it bends left before the farm then angles down the hillside, avoiding paths off left and right. At the bottom cross Mill Clough and continue up the track to Madscar Farm. Before the farmyard branch left for the steep surfaced lane above the buildings. Keep going beyond the hairpin to reach Overton Hall Farm.

❻ Just before the farm buildings take the wide and sometimes muddy track on your right. Follow this direct and unmade route, called Whiteleas Road, across the pasture and all the way down to Taxal. Go through the gate and along the lane until just before the Church of St James.

❼ Turn right down a steep, surfaced track beside the graveyard. At the bottom take the short path on the left to cross the river by a footbridge. On the far bank go right, then immediately left, for the steep track up to the start.

Walk 11: Combs Reservoir

COMBS RESERVOIR AND ACROSS DICKIE'S MEADOW

A quiet corner of Derbyshire, between the Goyt and Chapel-en-le-Frith.

Combs lies off the road between Chapel-en-le-Frith and Whaley Bridge and beneath the sombre crag-fringed slopes of Combs Moss. This is a fine little corner of north-west Derbyshire, tucked away from the crowds of Castleton and Hathersage.

Dickie's Meadow
The route starts by the west side of the dam on a narrow path between the lake and Meveril Brook. Beyond the reservoir the path tucks under the railway, which brings to mind a mysterious story concerning Ned Dixon, who lived in nearby Tunstead Farm. Ned, or Dickie as he was known, was brutally murdered by his cousin. Locals say his spirit lived on in his skull, which was left outside to guard against intruders.

Combs
A lane winds into the village of Combs, where a handful of stone-built cottages are centred on the welcoming Beehive Inn. Combs' most famous son is Herbert Froode. He made his name in automotive engineering as one of the inventors of the brake lining. Starting out in the early 1890s he developed woven cotton brakes for horse-drawn wagons, but his ideas didn't really take off until 1897 when the first motor buses emerged. Froode applied his knowledge of brakes to this much greater challenge and by the end of the century had won a contract to supply brake linings for the new London omnibuses. Ferodo, his company, is an anagram of his surname.

Final Views
Through the village the route takes to the hillsides. Now Combs Reservoir, which is spread beneath your feet, looks every bit a natural lake. Beyond it are the plains of Manchester and the hazy blue West Pennine horizon.

This very pleasing walk ends as it starts, by the shores of the reservoir. If you look along the line of the dam towards the right of two farms, you'll see where Dickie lived. He's probably watching you, too.

Combs Reservoir

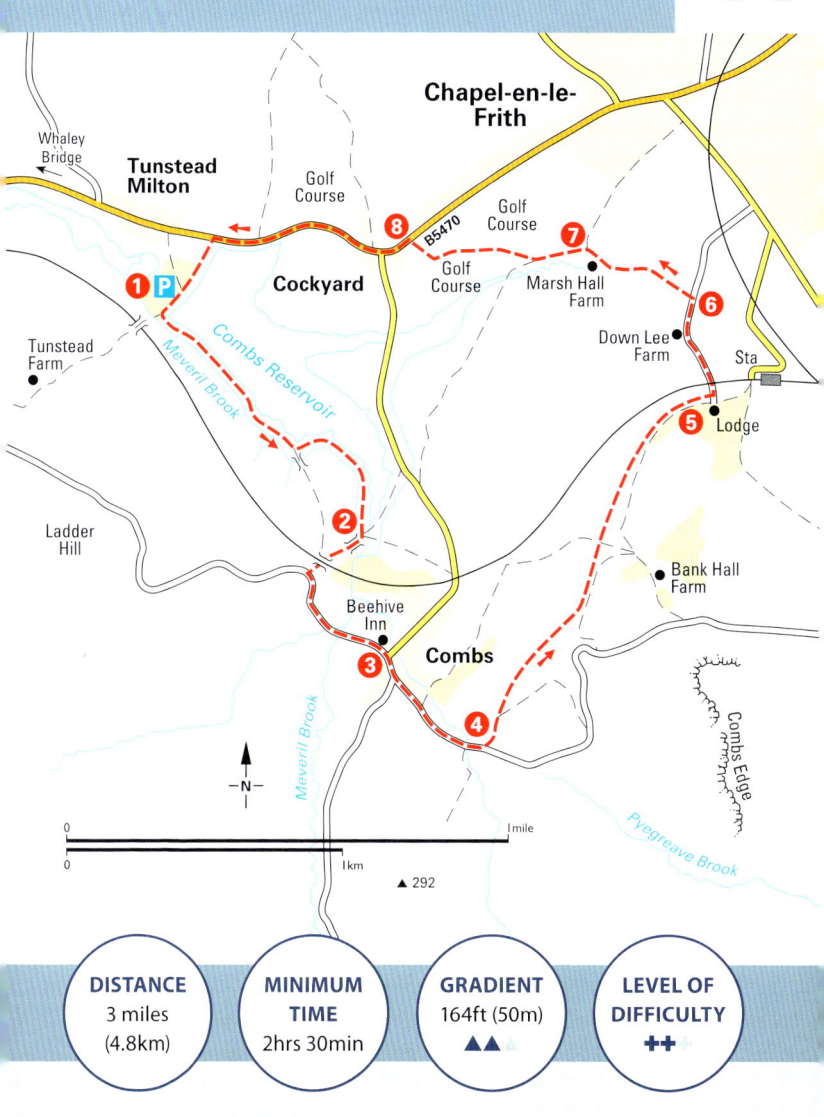

Walk 11

DISTANCE	MINIMUM TIME	GRADIENT	LEVEL OF DIFFICULTY
3 miles (4.8km)	2hrs 30min	164ft (50m) ▲▲	++

PATHS Can be muddy, quite a few stiles
LANDSCAPE Lakes, meadows, and high moors
SUGGESTED MAP OS Explorer OL24 White Peak
START/FINISH Grid reference: SK 033797
DOG FRIENDLINESS Farmland – dogs should be kept on leads
PARKING Combs Reservoir car park
PUBLIC TOILETS None on route

Walk 11: Combs Reservoir

WALK 11 DIRECTIONS

❶ Follow the path from the dam along the reservoir's western shore, ignoring the first footbridge over Meveril Brook.

❷ As the reservoir narrows the path traverses small fields, then comes to another footbridge over the brook. This time cross it and head south across another field. Beyond a foot tunnel under the Buxton line railway, the path reaches a narrow hedge-lined country lane. Turn left along the lane into Combs village.

❸ Past the Beehive Inn in the village centre, take the lane straight ahead, then the left fork, signposted to Dove Holes. This climbs out of the village towards Combs Edge.

> 🍴 **EATING AND DRINKING**
> The Beehive Inn at Combs is a splendid little pub serving fine bar meals. Alternatively, there's the more formal Hanging Gate Inn at Cockyard.

❹ Take the second footpath on the left, which begins at a muddy clearing just beyond Millway Cottage. Go through the stile and climb on a partially slabbed path and then uphill across pasture with the wall on your right. Away to the right is the huge comb of Pygreave Brook. Climb the pathless spur and go through gateways in the next two boundary walls before following a wall on the right. Ignore a gate in this wall – that's a path to Bank Hall Farm – but stay with the narrow path raking across rough grassy hillslopes with the railway line and the reservoir below left.

❺ The path comes down to a track that runs alongside the railway line. This joins a lane just short of the Lodge. Turn left to go under the railway and north to Down Lee Farm.

❻ Turn left through a kissing gate 200yds (183m) beyond the farmhouse. The signposted path follows an overgrown hedge towards Marsh Hall Farm. The fields can become very boggy on the final approaches. When you reach the farm complex turn right over a stile and follow a vehicle track heading north-west.

❼ After 200yds (183m) turn left on a field path that heads west to a stile at the edge of the Chapel-en-le-Frith golf course. Waymarking arrows show the way across the fairway. The stile marking the exit from the golf course is 300yds (274m) short of the clubhouse. Then cross a field to reach the B5470.

❽ Turn left along the road (there's a pavement on the far side), and follow it past the Hanging Gate pub at Cockyard. After passing the entrance to the sailing club, turn left to cross over the dam of Combs Reservoir and return to the car park.

Hay Dale

Walk 12

A NATURE RESERVE IN MINIATURE

The wild flowers and butterflies of Hay Dale make for a delightful nature walk.

The Northern Brown Argus is not, at first sight, the most showy of butterflies. It's small and dark brown in colour, with variable orange or white spots on the edges of its wings, although in flight it seems almost silvery. You can find it on sheltered, limestone slopes where it feasts on the common rock rose, a low, evergreen trailing plant that flowers yellow between May and July.

Limestone Dales

Sadly the Northern Brown Argus is also dwindling in number, the scattered colonies across the north of England becoming fewer and fewer. One place where it's still doing well, however, is the unspoilt little valley of Hay Dale near Tideswell, rich in limestone-loving herbs and wild flowers like the common rock rose. Hay Dale is one of five separate limestone valleys that together make up Derbyshire Dales National Nature Reserve (the others are Monk's, Cressbrook, Lathkill and Long dales). These largely untouched limestone dales are usually narrow and in places wooded, their thin grassy slopes often punctured by scree or bare rock. Hay Dale is perhaps the most delicate and certainly the smallest, easily accessible but bursting with wild flowers that carpet the dale floor and gentle eastern slopes in spring and early summer.

Nature Reserve

The walk begins by skirting the top of Hay Dale along field paths, offering glimpses into the shallow green valley below. Before long it drops down into the National Nature Reserve, following an old mining track along the dale bottom. The final stage is back up a quiet country lane, and even there look out for nature. The grassy bank on the left has been designated a 'Road Verge Reserve', simply a roadside location that local people and landowners have identified as being rich in wild flowers. The Peak District National Park is keen to help species like ox-eye daisy, field scabious and meadow cranesbill, all of which have declined over the last 50 years, by encouraging mowing at appropriate times (so that the flowers are able to drop their seeds) and organising volunteers to control invasive scrub and bracken.

Walk 12 Hay Dale

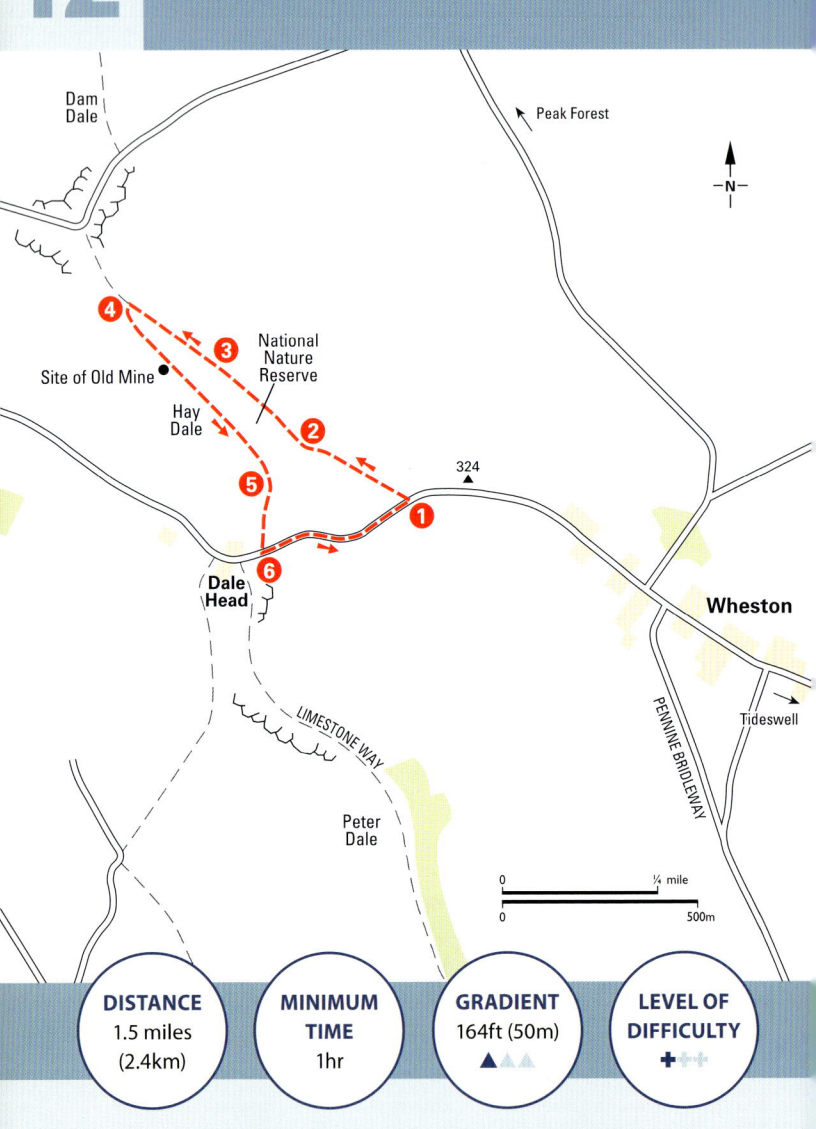

DISTANCE	MINIMUM TIME	GRADIENT	LEVEL OF DIFFICULTY
1.5 miles (2.4km)	1hr	164ft (50m)	

PATHS Firm in dale, but potentially muddy farm track at start, 5 stiles
LANDSCAPE Flower-rich limestone dale and grassland
SUGGESTED MAP OS Explorer OL24 White Peak
START/FINISH Grid reference: SK 127767
DOG FRIENDLINESS On lead around livestock **PARKING** Wide grass verge at top of lane **PUBLIC TOILETS** Nearest at Tideswell **NOTE** There are some small cliffs on the upper eastern slopes of Hay Dale, so keep an eye on young children

48 40 Short Walks in the Peak District

Hay Dale
Walk 12

WALK 12 DIRECTIONS

1 Go over the wall stile, next to the footpath sign, a few paces from the roadside verge (parking). Walk up the short grassy bank to cross the stile next to the gate and proceed along the level farm track with the wall on your left.

2 Just before the track ends at a wide metal gate go over the wall stile on the left. Ahead is a long, narrow field. Aim for the far left corner, keeping Hay Dale below on your left. Eventually you reach a wooden stile. Cross this and enter the National Nature Reserve, next to a display board and map.

3 Turn right and follow a faint path slanting gradually down the hillside, among trees and rocky outcrops. It passes through a small gap in the rocks and descends to the partly wooded dale below, where you reach the clear grassy track along the dale bottom.

4 Turn left and follow the obvious, well-walked route south-eastwards along the foot of the dale, initially through some thin tree cover. Go through a gate and out into the open dry valley, with the grassy sides rising sharply above.

5 After 0.5 miles (800m) you cross a stile at the edge of the reserve by another noticeboard. Continue along the easy, flat path through a short but narrow walled field until you reach a stile by the road at Dale Head.

6 Cross the stile and turn left. Walk up the narrow, curving lane to the top of the dale to reach your car.

> **IN THE AREA**
> Freshfields Donkey Village, near Peak Forest, not only rescues and cares for unwanted donkeys but it also uses the animals to work with children with special needs. The centre is open to visitors from March to September and includes a small tea room.

> **EATING AND DRINKING**
> The village of Tideswell has a range of pubs and tea rooms, the latter including the Vanilla Kitchen on Queen Street. Also visit the award-winning Tindalls Bakery and Delicatessen (opposite the church), which sells a great range of local produce and makes fresh rolls and sandwiches to order.

> **ON THE WALK**
> When you reach the bottom of the dale and turn left (Point **4**), you are walking in the footsteps of former miners. A short railway used to run along here, serving a calcite mine that was worked intermittently last century. Before you reach the gate across the path you can see the opening of the mine on the left, sealed up long ago.

Walk 13 Castleton

CASTLES AND CAVERNS

Castleton is where the limestone of the White Peak and the shales and gritstone of the Dark Peak collide.

Castleton is the last settlement before the Hope Valley narrows and squeezes into the rocky ravine of Winnats. It's a bustling tourist town with a history evident back to Norman times, and a geology that has been responsible for many of its successes and most of its failures. At Castleton the shales and gritstone of the Dark Peak and the limestone plateaux of the White Peak meet. Here countless generations of miners have dug their shafts and enlarged the natural caves which riddle the bedrock in search of precious ore. Here too, they built an ambitious road that eventually succumbed to the landslides of Mam Tor, the 'Shivering Mountain'.

Boat Trip

After threading your way through Castleton's back streets, the first cavern of the day is Peak Cavern. You can walk right up to its entrance at the foot of vertical cliffs, 280ft (85m) high, in a natural gorge overlooking the town.

Soon you're out across the fields and heading for Speedwell Cavern at the foot of the Winnats Pass. A fascinating boat trip takes you down the canal to a landing stage just short of the 'Bottomless Pit', named because the spoil thrown in by miners made no impression on its depth.

Blue John

From here you climb the hillside at the head of the valley to reach Treak Cliff Cavern, then on to Blue John. The floodlights of the chambers show off the old river galleries with crystalline waterfalls, and a fascinating array of stalagmites and stalactites. Dominating the view from the cavern entrance is Mam Tor, below which is the crumbling tarmac of the ill-fated road and the huge shale landslides that have plagued the valley for centuries.

The return to Castleton is down the dramatic Winnats Pass, a deep and narrow grassy valley that squeezes between massive limestone cliffs and pinnacles. Some believe it to be a long collapsed cave system; others hold it to be a ravine in the coral reef laid down around 320 million years ago when a shallow tropical lagoon covered this area.

ple
Castleton

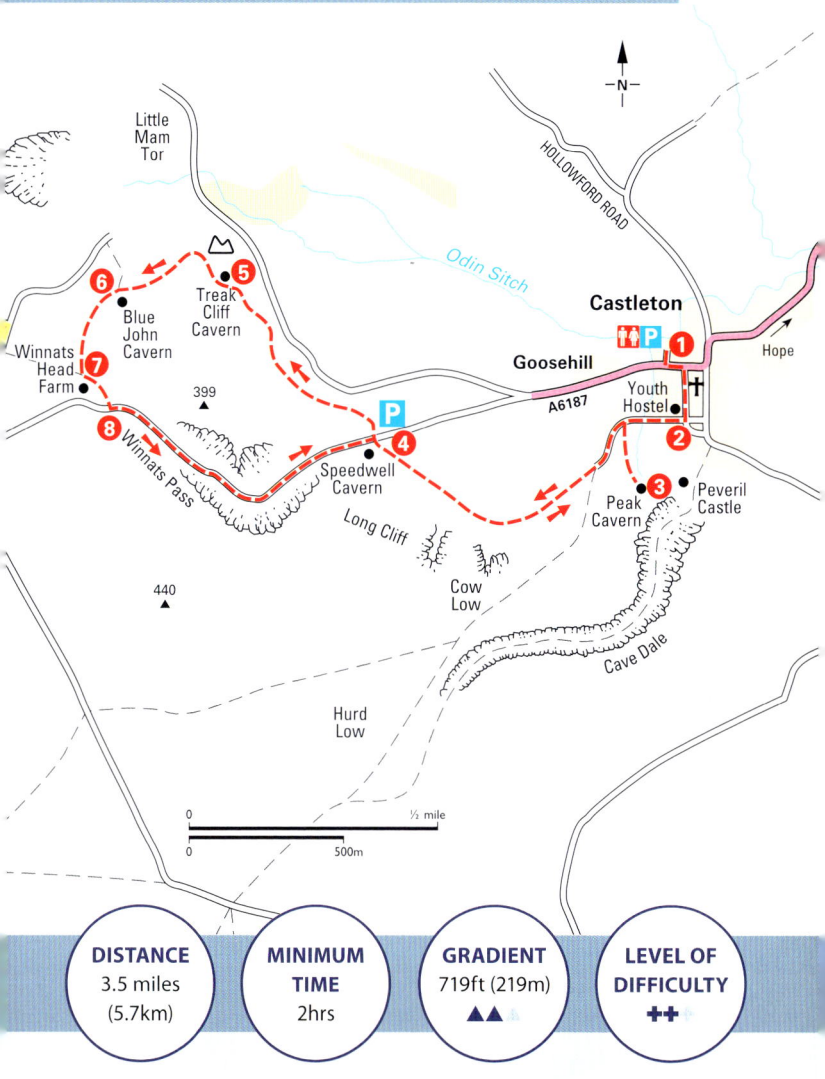

Walk 13

DISTANCE 3.5 miles (5.7km)	**MINIMUM TIME** 2hrs	**GRADIENT** 719ft (219m) ▲▲	**LEVEL OF DIFFICULTY** ✦✦

PATHS The steep grassy hillsides can be slippery in wet or wintry conditions
LANDSCAPE Limestone ravines and pastureland
SUGGESTED MAP OS Explorer OL1 Dark Peak
START/FINISH Grid reference: SK 149829
DOG FRIENDLINESS Much of this is National Trust land, where dogs are requested to be on lead **PARKING** Main Castleton pay car park by visitor centre **PUBLIC TOILETS** At car park

Castleton 51

Walk 13: Castleton

WALK 13 DIRECTIONS

1 From the car park turn left along the main street then turn right up Castle Street, passing the church to reach the youth hostel on the right. The entrance to Peveril Castle is straight ahead.

2 Turn right immediately after the youth hostel on to a narrow lane. Turn left on the far side of the bridge for the lane to the entrance to Peak Cavern.

3 Retrace your steps and fork left by Rose Cottage to return to the lane, called Goosehill. Turn left and follow it uphill. It becomes unsurfaced and after a gate go out along a path along the bottom of a slope, next to a wall on your right. Follow it all the way round to Speedwell Cavern.

4 Cross over the road for the public footpath to Treak Cliff Cavern opposite. Don't drop down through a wall opening but go straight ahead, passing to the left of a small wood. Join the surfaced path up to reach the cavern entrance.

5 Follow the signposted public footpath around the back of the buildings and on across the high, open hillside on a clear path. At the top go through the left of two gates and on to Blue John Cavern.

6 Go past the entrance and on through a gate for the footpath up across the grassy hillside. Towards the top, aim for the public footpath sign by the wall in front of Winnats Head Farm.

7 Turn left and follow the outer edge of the farm down to the road. Don't go through the gate but instead go left, along the inside of the wall, to a gate further down.

8 Now follow the wide grassy strip beside the road all the way down Winnats Pass. At the bottom is Treak Cliff Cavern. Turn right after this for the footpath back to Castleton.

> **ON THE WALK**
> Treak Cliff Cavern is one of the best places to see fossils. In the limestone you can study the remains of sea creatures that accumulated in the bed of a tropical sea 320 million years ago.

> **EATING AND DRINKING**
> To complete your round-up of all the local places containing the word 'castle', try The Castle in Castle Street, which serves food throughout the day, or The George just a few doors along.

> **IN THE AREA**
> Besides the caverns seen along the way, try and make time for Peveril Castle, cared for by English Heritage. Along with a well-preserved Norman keep it offers wonderful views up Cave Dale and over the village.

Opposite: Looking toward Mam Tor

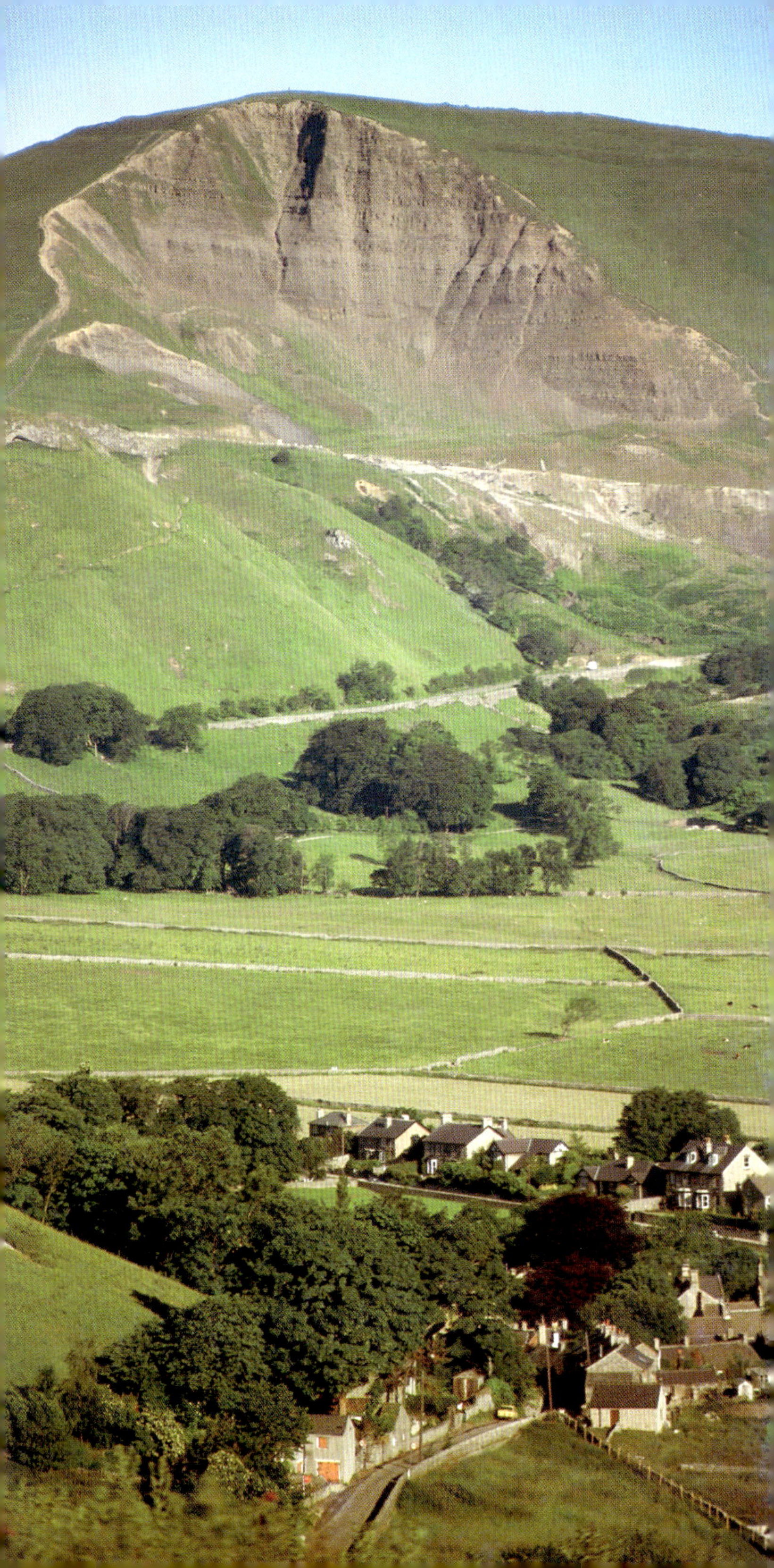

Walk 14: Bretton Clough

BRETTON'S GREEN AND HIDDEN VALLEY

Explore the secretive Bretton Clough tucked between the moors and a dramatic airy ridge.

Bretton Clough is a sheltered valley of woodland and open, bracken-covered slopes, a green oasis sandwiched between the harsh, dark upland of Abney Moor and Eyam Moor. A 'clough' is a local term for a small, steep-sided valley, typically found in the gritstone moors of the Dark Peak.

Barrel Inn

The walk begins at the Barrel Inn, which for over 250 years has been serving weary travellers journeying along the packhorse routes, turnpike road and footpaths that cross Eyam Edge. At 1,247ft high (380m) above sea level, the Barrel is the highest pub in Derbyshire, enjoying superlative views southwards over the heart of the Peak District. (Incidentally, the highest pub in the Peak District is the Cat and Fiddle at 1,683ft/513m, which lies in Cheshire.) It's said that on a clear day you can see five counties; and for those with exceptional vision the interpretation board outside the pub indicates the direction of London – a mere 142 miles (228km) away!

Lush Valley

You can savour the views as you stroll along the top of the edge, noting the village of Eyam immediately below (see Walk 16) and the huge quarries beyond it. The ridge across the horizon about 3 miles (4.8km) to the south is Longstone Edge (Walk 20). Soon you swing north and make your way gradually down to Bretton Clough via a small side valley. You can see how it's squeezed between the surrounding moorland, the rich greens of its lush vegetation contrasting with the darker and more sombre colours of the land above. This concealment has proved useful in the past. In 1745, local farmers drove their cattle into Bretton Clough to hide them from Bonnie Prince Charlie's Highland army as they marched south on their way to Derby.

Bretton Clough was once home to several farmsteads, but all that's left are a few ruined buildings. You pass one of these as you make your way through the valley, now a peaceful place and rich in birdlife, especially the woods of oak and birch that you climb through on your way back up to the hamlet.

Bretton Clough

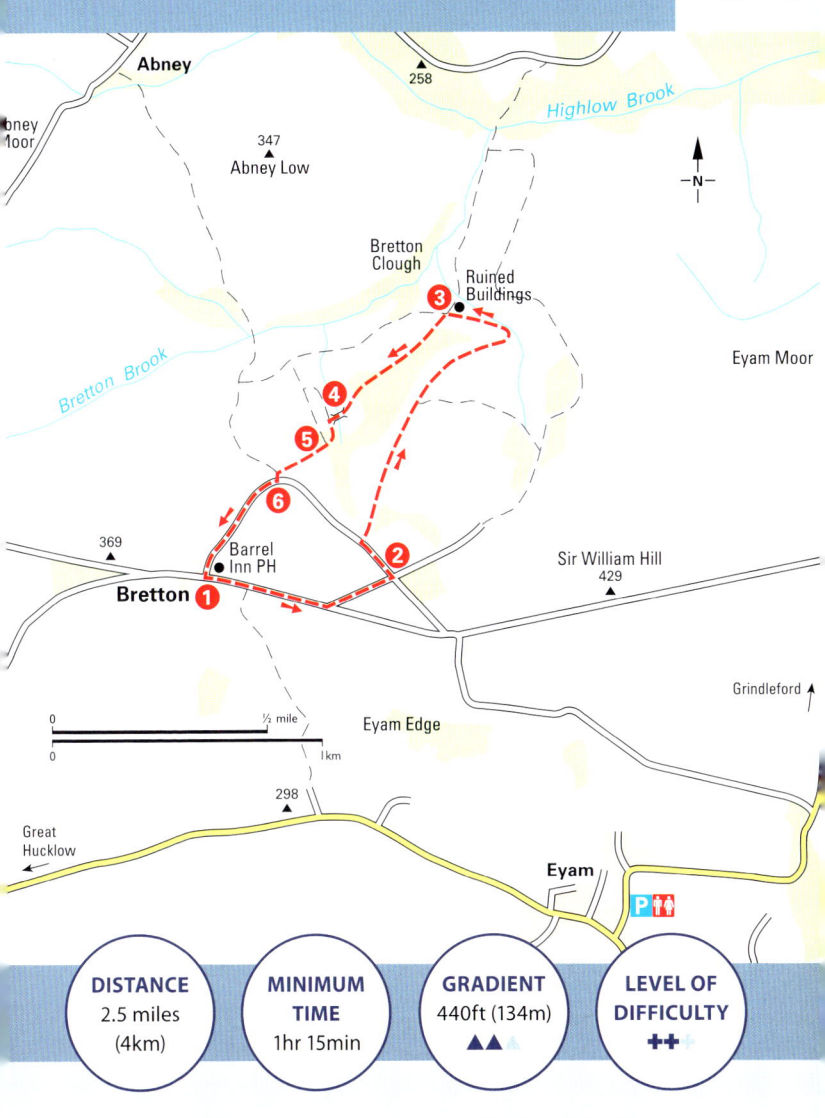

Walk 14

DISTANCE	MINIMUM TIME	GRADIENT	LEVEL OF DIFFICULTY
2.5 miles (4km)	1hr 15min	440ft (134m) ▲▲	++

PATHS Lanes, grassy tracks and woodland paths, 2 stiles
LANDSCAPE High moorland and sheltered, part-wooded valley
SUGGESTED MAP OS Explorer OL24 White Peak
START/FINISH Grid reference: SK 202778
DOG FRIENDLINESS On lead around livestock which graze the valley
PARKING Roadside parking near Barrel Inn
PUBLIC TOILETS Nearest at Eyam

Bretton Clough 55

Walk 14: Bretton Clough

WALK 14 DIRECTIONS

1 Facing the front door of the Barrel Inn, turn right and walk up the lane along the top of Eyam Edge. After 550yds (503m), before a small lay-by, take a green walled track on the left that slants across the fields.

2 At a crossroads of tracks turn left. In 0.25 miles (400m) turn right signposted 'Bretton Clough'. Follow this footpath past a small plantation and out across the hillside next to a tumbledown wall. Go through successive gates then curve round a side valley, still heading downhill, until you finally reach some dilapidated buildings partly hidden by trees.

3 Keeping the buildings on your right, continue along the grassy track, which is joined by another, across the open and bumpy land for just over 0.25 miles (400m). When you reach woodland drop down and go over a stile.

4 Follow the path across a small stream and up the far slope. The path bends sharply left, through a gate, and continues through the trees steadily up the valley, steepening towards the top when it winds round to the right.

5 When you emerge from the trees at another path, near a bench, go left. Just before a second bench turn right, over a stile, for a fenced path uphill. Pass to the right of a house to reach the lane.

6 Turn right and follow the surfaced lane back to the Barrel Inn, with glorious views of Abney Moor and Bretton Clough over your right shoulder.

EATING AND DRINKING

The Barrel Inn is open lunchtime and evenings for food and drink, including light snacks and hot meals. Walkers and dogs are welcome and there's outside seating, including a covered area, although if the wind is blowing the indoor log fire might be more appealing.

ON THE WALK

When you reach the bottom of Bretton Clough you'll notice the bumpy and uneven valley floor. This is the result of landslips long ago, when the soft and unstable shale layered between the harder gritstone gave way and caused the land to slump.

IN THE AREA

To the south-west of Bretton, at the foot of the edge, is the Hucklow Lead Rake Trail. This short walking route traces the vein of lead ore which once made the Great Hucklow area so important for mining. Today you can see how the industry developed, what it took to extract this valuable commodity and inspect recent excavations.

WOODS AND WATERFALLS AT PADLEY GORGE

Noisy cascades, hidden dells and weirdly shaped trees give Padley Gorge a wonderfully Tolkiensque feel.

Burbage Brook begins its life quite sedately, high up on the heather moors above Sheffield, and as it enters the National Trust's Longshaw Estate it's a pleasant stream just begging for a paddle or perhaps a picnic on its irresistible grassy banks. Then, all of a sudden, it disappears into the woods and plunges down the side of the Derwent Valley towards Grindleford and it takes on a wholly different appearance.

Deep Ravine

The walk traces the route of the brook as it cascades downhill, forming waterfalls and occasional rapids, and carving out a deep ravine among the trees. Indeed, Padley Gorge is renowned for its historic woodland, the native oak and birch a remnant of what must have once cloaked much of the wider valley. And what's left is wonderfully atmospheric, with many of the trees that cling to the rocky hillside twisted into shapes that wouldn't be out of place in one of J R R Tolkien's books.

You may not see a Hobbitt but what you probably will see are woodland birds. Apart from residents like great tits, treecreepers and nuthatches, the woods attract summer visitors such as pied flycatchers, wood warblers and redstarts; while downstream look out for dippers and grey wagtails.

Padley Chapel

At the foot of the gorge the route emerges at Upper Padley, where there's a brief excursion to inspect Padley Chapel, a barn-like building dating from the Middle Ages. Two Catholic priests were discovered hiding here in 1588 at a time of religious intolerance, and were subsequently sentenced to death for high treason. Their martyrdom is remembered by pilgrimages, and the chapel is open for visitors on Wednesday and Sunday afternoons in summer. Once you've clambered back up the gorge and emerged from the woods, pause to admire a new wooden footbridge. It was made out of a single oak in 2010 by local wood-worker and ex-National Trust forester Robin Wood (who also made the beech bridge visited on Walk 6).

Walk 15 — Padley Gorge

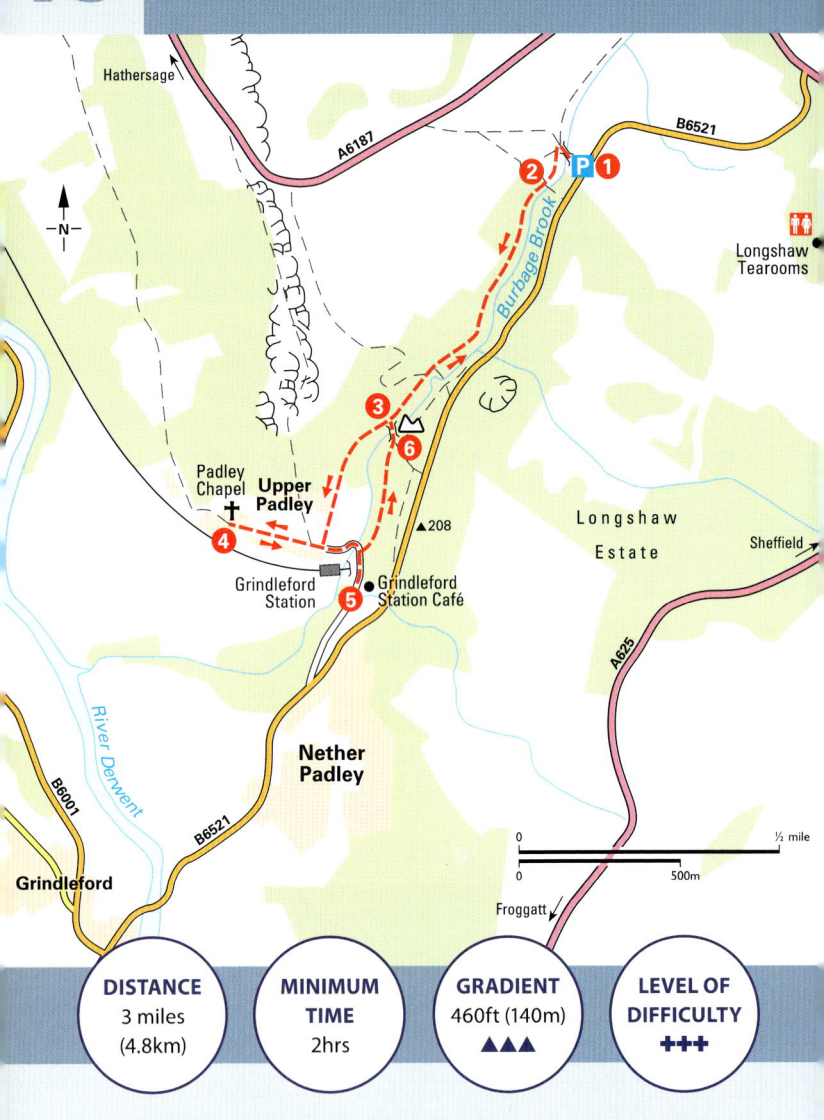

| **DISTANCE** 3 miles (4.8km) | **MINIMUM TIME** 2hrs | **GRADIENT** 460ft (140m) ▲▲▲ | **LEVEL OF DIFFICULTY** +++ |

PATHS Mix of firm tracks and rough woodland paths, often rocky and sometimes muddy **LANDSCAPE** River gorge with steeply wooded hillside **SUGGESTED MAP** OS Explorer OL24 White Peak **START/FINISH** Grid reference: SK 257799 **DOG FRIENDLINESS** The National Trust request dogs under close control at all times and on lead between April and July **PARKING** Defined roadside strip on B6521 above the top of the gorge **PUBLIC TOILETS** Nearest at Longshaw visitor centre

58   40 Short Walks in the Peak District

Padley Gorge — Walk 15

WALK 15 DIRECTIONS

1 From the roadside gate go down to the path and follow it to the right, past the signpost and cross Burbage Brook by the footbridge. Turn left and follow the riverside path downstream until you meet a gate into woodland.

> ### IN THE AREA
> For a very different kind of outing, try the David Mellor visitor centre at nearby Hathersage (open daily). It's both a showcase and shop for one of Sheffield's top designers of high-class cutlery and kitchen ware, and includes a design museum and café.

2 Follow this clear but bumpy path along the upper slopes of the wooded gorge, with the cascading brook increasingly far below on the left. Ignore paths off left and right until you come to a gently rising section of shallow stone steps.

3 Continue on, up the rocky path, and staying on the main route you eventually begin to drop down to the edge of the wood. Go through the gate at the bottom and down an unmade residential lane. At the bottom turn right to reach Padley Chapel.

4 Retrace your steps along the level lane, going straight on at the junction and then past Padley Mill and over the brook to reach the café on the far side of the railway bridge.

5 Go back across the railway until, just before the bridge across the brook, go right through a wall gap by the National Trust sign for Padley Gorge. There are lots of paths up the rough, wooded hillside, but stay close to, or in sight of the brook on the left.

6 After about 0.25 miles (400m) drop down to cross the brook by a footbridge at the bottom of the ravine. Go up the steep, switchback path on the far bank and rejoin the outward route at Point **3**. Turn right and follow this back to the top of the gorge.

> ### ON THE WALK
> If you find a shady spot to picnic in Padley Gorge just keep an eye on where you're sitting. One of the wood's special residents is the hairy wood ant; up to 0.5in (10mm) in length and responsible for the large mounds out of woodland matter you may see dotted about. They can also bite, so be warned!

> ### EATING AND DRINKING
> Grindleford Station Café, located at the bottom of Padley Gorge, has long been a favourite for outdoor types. It's the type of place where tea comes in pint mugs, plus there's a large area of outdoor seating which is ideal for dog walkers and muddy boots. The National Trust's tearooms at nearby Longshaw are also very good.

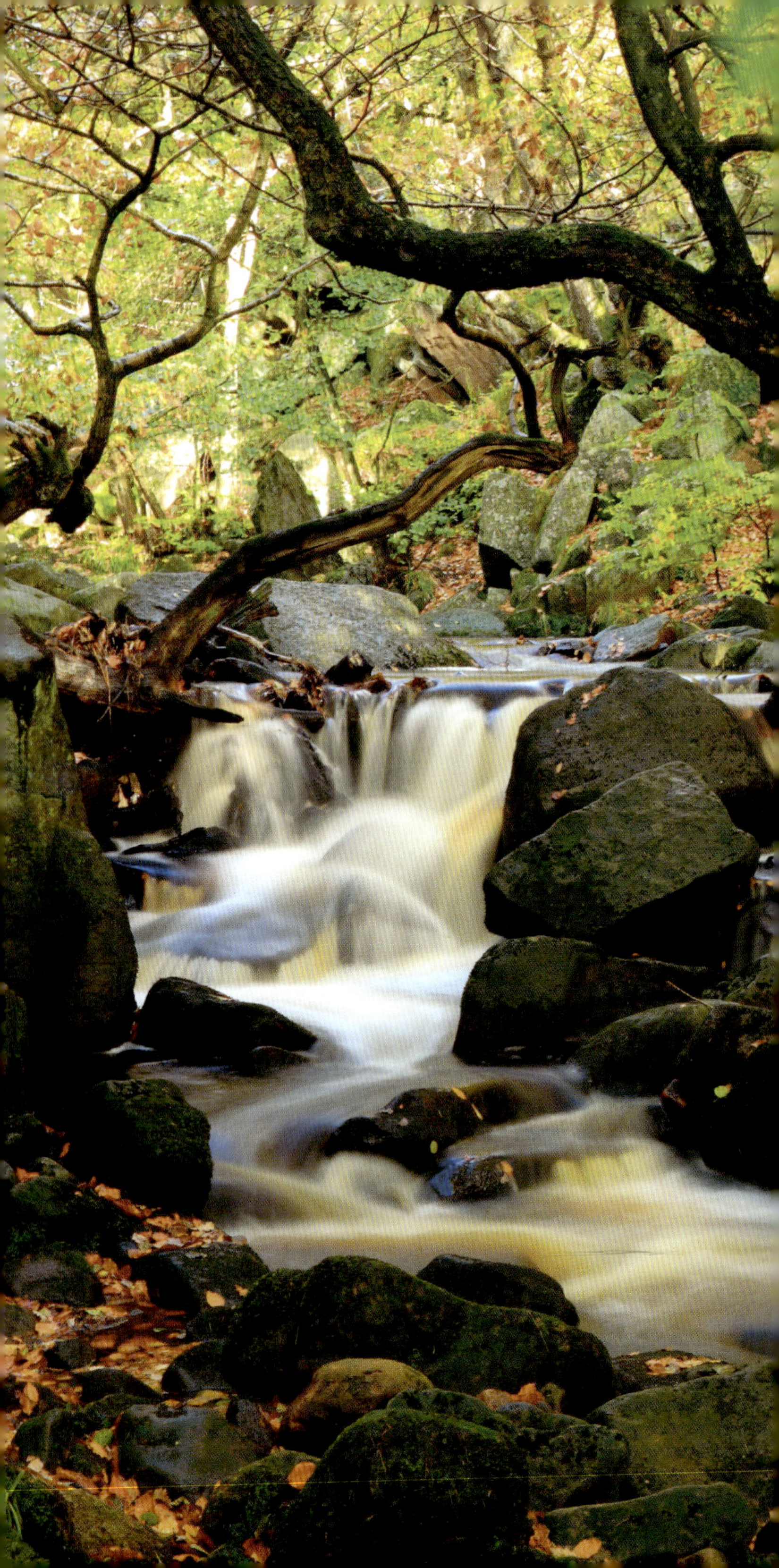

Burbage Brook flowing through Padley Gorge

Walk 16: Eyam

INFECTIOUS HISTORICAL CHARM AT EYAM

Best known as the self-sacrificing plague village, Eyam also boasts a rich and interesting history.

Eyam is best known as the community that went into a self-imposed quarantine when the plague arrived, desperately trying to prevent it from spreading throughout Derbyshire. It came to Eyam via a batch of infected cloth from London in summer 1665 and soon the local tailor's family was struck down. It quickly spread to the entire community and when it was over, 14 months later, it had claimed the lives of 260 villagers.

Drastic Action

It would be wrong, however, to think that Eyam's history began and ended with the plague. Early settlers were attracted by the plentiful supply of water, and in Eyam churchyard, for instance, there's a Saxon preaching cross from the 8th century. Since then, and in common with many other Peak District communities, farming and mining have been the two main occupations. Lead, barytes and fluorspar have all been all extracted at various times, but when a major works on the edge of the village closed some years ago it signalled a large-scale regeneration project which has resulted in housing and recreation facilities – all of which you can see at the end of the walk.

Historic Buildings

Eyam also has its fair share of interesting and beautiful old buildings. Eyam Hall, which you pass on Church Street, is an imposing Jacobean manor house whose farm buildings have been converted into a craft centre. In contrast, only a few paces along the street, is a simple terrace row of cottages, including the Plague Cottage where the 'visitation' (as it was called) first struck in Eyam.

Although there are plenty of interesting interpretation boards dotted around the village, your walk must either begin or end with a visit to Eyam Museum, which chronicles the entire history of the village. It's open Tuesday–Sunday, March–November. For a more detailed guide to the village buy a copy of *The Eyam Map*, produced by villagers as a special Millennium project and full of illustrated detail.

Eyam

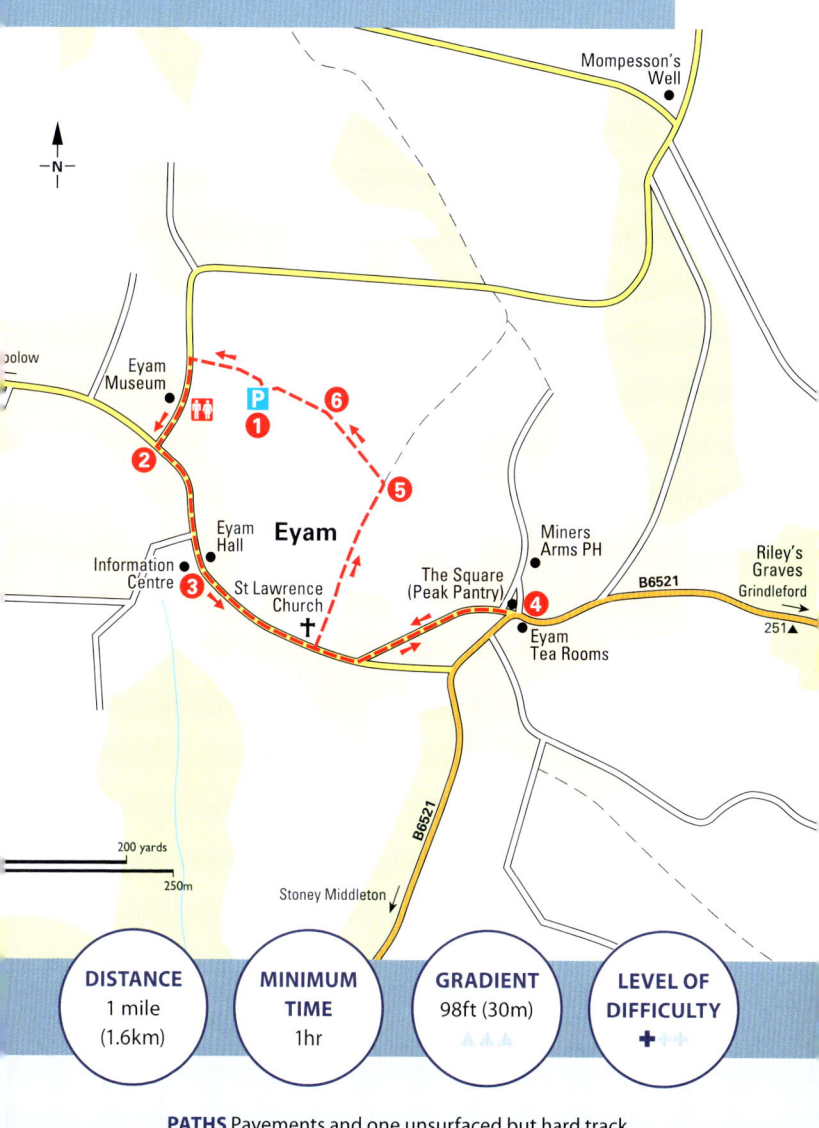

Walk 16

DISTANCE	MINIMUM TIME	GRADIENT	LEVEL OF DIFFICULTY
1 mile (1.6km)	1hr	98ft (30m)	+++

PATHS Pavements and one unsurfaced but hard track
LANDSCAPE Village street scene
SUGGESTED MAP OS Explorer OL24 White Peak
START/FINISH Grid reference: SK 216767
DOG FRIENDLINESS On lead on streets
PARKING Parish Council car park
PUBLIC TOILETS Near car park

Eyam 63

Walk 16: Eyam

WALK 16 DIRECTIONS

1 Go out of the Parish Council's free car park (not the District Council one just below, which charges) and turn left, down Hawkshill Road. Eyam Museum is on the right, which you can either visit now or at the end of the walk.

2 At the junction at the bottom of the road turn left. Walk along Church Street through the middle of the village. On the right, opposite Eyam Hall, is a seasonal information centre in the old market hall.

IN THE AREA
If you go up Hawkshill Road and follow it to the top of the steep hillside you come to Mompesson's Well (by the turning to Bretton). It was where food and other supplies were left for collection by the villagers, who in return paid with money they placed in the running water to be sanitised.

3 Continue along Church Street past the sheep roast, the Plague Cottage and the church. Just after the school fork left at the junction and follow the road down to The Square in the heart of the village.

ON THE WALK
Opposite Eyam Hall, on a small green, are Eyam stocks. At one time every town had to have this form of punishment which was meted out to miscreants who didn't obey the law. They would be locked in the stocks by their hands and feet for a specified time, usually several hours or more, and then subjected to the ridicule (or worse) of passers by.

4 After visiting the cafés or pub and inspecting the various interpretation boards, retrace your steps to St Helen's Church. Go right at the gate into the churchyard, signed 'public footpath', and either visit the church or follow the path around the building. Head for the exit at the north-eastern corner.

5 Go through the black swing gate and turn left for a dirt track uphill, with the graveyard on your left. Above on the right is a football pitch. At the top of this track you come to a gate.

6 Go through the gate, then a second, with the children's play area and the village cricket green on the left. Go straight on to reach the car park.

EATING AND DRINKING
Peak Pantry and Eyam Tea Rooms, both on The Square, are handy places at which to refuel. Peak Pantry also sells the mouth-watering Bradwell's ice cream, made locally in the Hope Valley. Eyam's sole pub, the Miners Arms, is located up Water Lane, next to Peak Pantry. It serves bar meals every lunchtime and evening and is open all day at weekends.

Baslow Edge Walk 17

LIFE ON THE EDGE

The gritstone outcrops of the Derwent Valley provide a high-level thrill for walkers and climbers.

The Derwent Valley dominates and defines the eastern side of the Peak District. Derbyshire's longest river rises on the remote moors of Bleaklow then flows 66 miles (106km) via Matlock to join the Trent south of Derby and so on to the North Sea. In its lower reaches the Derwent meanders over flat and gentle farmland, but through the Peak District the valley's high eastern rim sports a succession of dark, often continuous gritstone cliffs known as edges. Stanage, Froggatt, Curbar and Baslow edges provide wonderful viewpoints and exhilarating walking; but the exposed crags, cliffs and boulders have also made the area one of the foremost in England for climbing. The most popular location is Stanage Edge, above Hathersage.

Eagle Stone

Even on Baslow Edge, which for most climbers is rather tame by comparison, there may be one or two climbers practising their moves on the Eagle Stone. Mind you, this giant gritstone boulder, weathered into weird shapes and sitting quite alone amid the heather, has long been a source of challenge. In centuries past, the eager young men of Baslow used to climb unaided to the top to demonstrate their manly prowess and eligibility for marriage.

After visiting the Eagle Stone, this easy and straightforward walk across the moor visits another rocky highlight, but this time not entirely natural. Wellington's Monument was built in 1866 by a local doctor as a tribute to the Duke of Wellington, who had died a few years before. It complements the Nelson Monument erected on Birchen Edge, less than a mile (1.6km) to the south east. Curiously, near this particular stone obelisk are several huge (and quite natural) rocks shaped like the prows of ships and bearing the carved names of three of Nelson's ships – *Victory*, *Defiant* and *Soverin* (sic).

The return is along the edge itself, with outstanding views that are full of interest. To the south are the distinctive tree-lined avenues and parkland of Chatsworth; across the valley the quarried flanks of Longstone Edge; and below your feet the villages of Baslow, Curbar and Calver, laid out across the valley's green floor and with the River Derwent flowing between them.

Walk 17 Baslow Edge

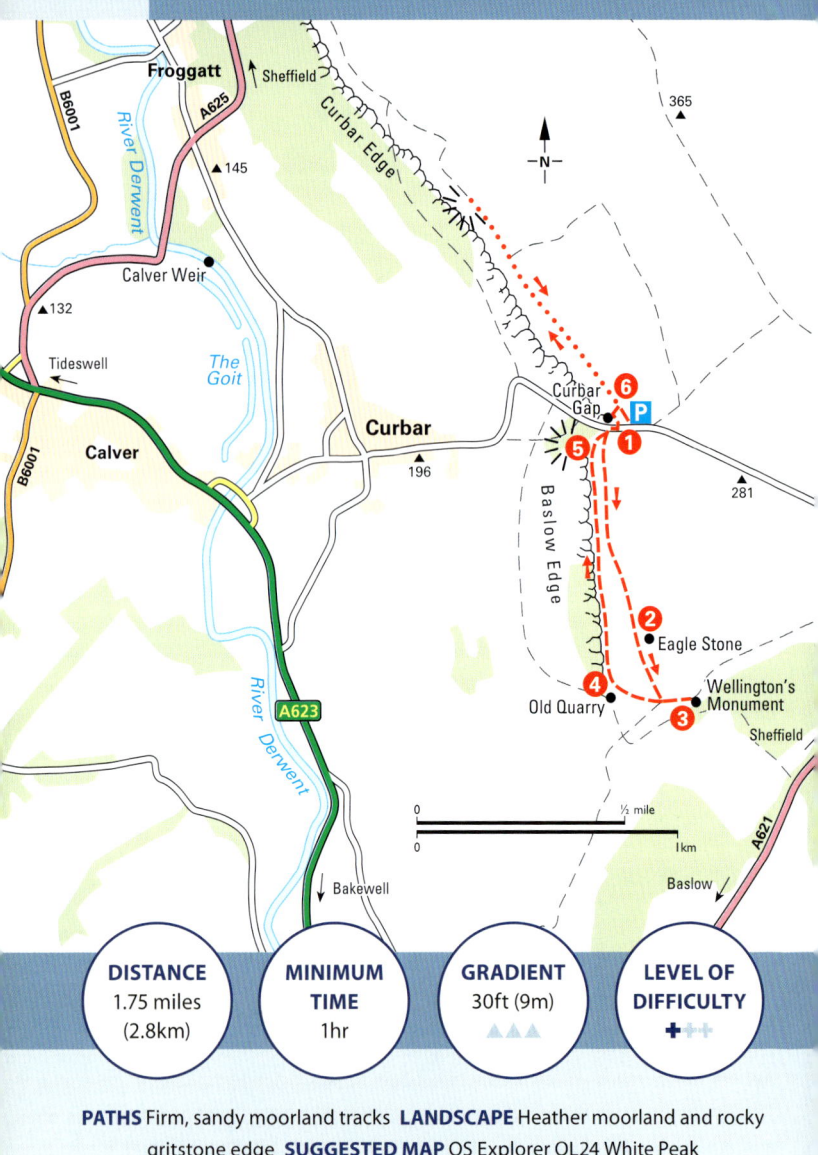

DISTANCE	**MINIMUM TIME**	**GRADIENT**	**LEVEL OF DIFFICULTY**
1.75 miles (2.8km)	1hr	30ft (9m)	+++

PATHS Firm, sandy moorland tracks **LANDSCAPE** Heather moorland and rocky gritstone edge **SUGGESTED MAP** OS Explorer OL24 White Peak **START/FINISH** Grid reference: SK 263747 **DOG FRIENDLINESS** On lead around cattle and calves which graze on Baslow Edge **PARKING** Peak Curbar Gap pay car park **PUBLIC TOILETS** Nearest at Baslow, by main car park **NOTE** Beware of sudden drops along Baslow Edge itself

66 40 Short Walks in the Peak District

Baslow Edge — Walk 17

WALK 17 DIRECTIONS

1 Follow the sign for Baslow Edge out of the car park and across the road on to a path. Go through the gate at the end and along a track out on to the moors, with the Derwent Valley to your right. Continue for 0.5 miles (800m) as far as the huge Eagle Stone.

2 Continue along the same path for another 250yds (229m) until you reach a junction of tracks at the edge of the moorland, where the ground falls away ahead. Turn left and walk the short distance to Wellington's Monument.

3 Turn round and walk back to the junction of routes. Here ignore the broad track heading gently down the slope on the left and instead go straight over for a narrow but obvious path up through bracken and heather. Continue on this above a small quarry, closed long ago and now overgrown.

4 The occasionally bumpy path now follows the moorland edge, via rocky outcrops and ledges. Continue across an open grassy area as far as a small, walled viewing point.

> **IN THE AREA**
> On the River Derwent a mile (1.6km) north of Curbar, the Grade II listed Calver Weir was built in the 1840s to power Richard Arkwright's cotton mills at Calver. After years of decay, a £1.8m restoration project was completed in 2010.

5 Follow the semi-surfaced path from the viewpoint back towards Curbar Gap and the gate for the path back to the car park, but this time go through the left-hand gate. Descend to cross the road for the track opposite and walk uphill as far as a white gate.

6 Turn right for a short path back to the car park, or go through the gate and follow the path for a further 0.25 miles (400m) on to Curbar Edge.

> **EATING AND DRINKING**
> The Café on the Green at nearby Baslow, by the wide triangular green opposite the car park, is open every day throughout the year and is very popular with walkers, serving a good selection of hot and cold food. It's a clean, wholesome and unfussy place, with a warm welcome for families.

> **ON THE WALK**
> When you reach the Eagle Stone don't be alarmed if you meet a young man or woman standing on a mat rubbing chalk into their hands. They are about to go 'bouldering', a style of rock climbing without ropes that involves very short ascents of low rocks or boulders where the focus is on agility and technique. (And, yes, they sometimes fall off – hence the mats.)

Walk 18: Linacre Reservoirs

LINACRE'S PEACEFUL RETREAT

Three quiet, tree-lined reservoirs are secreted away between the Chatsworth moors and Chesterfield.

It's easy to forget, as you look across Linacre and the valley of Holme Brook today, that Chesterfield is only a few miles away. This tranquil combe, sheltered from the west winds by the high heather moors, has three small reservoirs surrounded by attractive woodland. Linacre means arable land where flax is grown and, as early as the 13th century, linen from that flax was manufactured in the valley. But until the mid-19th century this was no more than an agricultural backwater of north-east Derbyshire.

Good Supply

It was the growth of Chesterfield and the Derbyshire coalfields, which brought the valley to notice. Here was a good supply of water, fed by those moors to the east. The reservoirs were built one by one between 1855 and 1904 in an attempt to supply these ever-growing requirements. Until 1909, when they built the filter beds, water was pumped direct from the reservoirs to consumers' homes.

If you've parked in the middle car park, you're standing above the ruins of two great buildings. Not much is known about the older Linacre Hall other than its mention in old charters, but the three-storey mansion of Linacre House was once home to Dr Thomas Linacre (1460–1524), who was president of the Royal College of Surgeons and physician to both Henry VIII and the young Mary, Queen of Scots.

About two thirds of the trees at Linacre are broadleaved, mainly sycamore, beech, oak and ash, while the remaining third are larch, pine and spruce. Hidden in the woods you may discover the remains of some old Q-holes. These were crudely dug pits of about 5ft (1.5m) in diameter where timber was once burned for use in the smelting of lead ore.

On the northern side of the top reservoir the route takes to a long boardwalk above the water's edge, which allows for a bird's eye view (in every sense). You'll almost certainly see moorhens, coots and mallards, perhaps even grebes or a sleek black cormorant, and maybe some of the migrating wildfowl that frequently visit.

Linacre Reservoirs

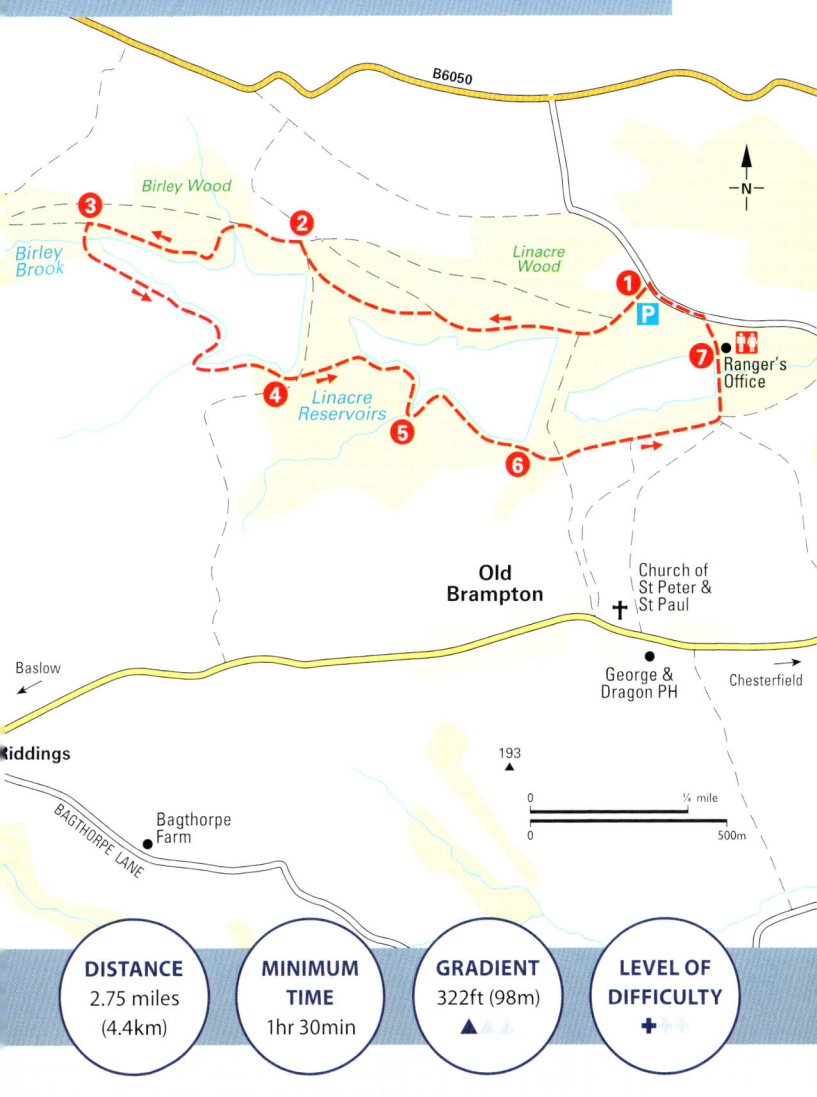

Walk 18

DISTANCE	MINIMUM TIME	GRADIENT	LEVEL OF DIFFICULTY
2.75 miles (4.4km)	1hr 30min	322ft (98m) ▲	✦✦✦

PATHS Mostly firm, but waterside paths can be muddy after rain, two long flights of steps **LANDSCAPE** Enclosed, wooded valley
SUGGESTED MAP OS Explorer OL24 White Peak
START/FINISH Grid reference: SK 336727
DOG FRIENDLINESS Good, but on lead in conservation areas around top reservoir **PARKING** Linacre Woods car park
PUBLIC TOILETS Near car park by Ranger's office

Linacre Reservoirs 69

Walk 18: Chesterfield & Linacre Reservoirs

WALK 18 DIRECTIONS

1 From the bottom of the lowest car park go down the steps into the woods. After about 100yds (91m) turn right along a waymarked bridleway. Approaching the dam of the middle reservoir fork right on the wide track and proceed westwards, with the reservoir through the trees on your left.

2 When you reach the dam of the upper reservoir stay on the main track as it swings right, up a few steps, and on along the wide wooded track above the shoreline. Dropping down to cross an inlet, go across the lower of the two footbridges for a concessionary path through woodland above the water.

3 At the end of the reservoir turn left on to a wooden footbridge over Birley Brook. Continue on the waterside route around the reservoir's northern and western shores, including a section of boardwalk and another bridge and steps. After reaching an area of pines you come to a junction of routes at the end of the dam of the top reservoir.

4 Ignore the main track as it swings right and go straight ahead on a path, waymarked as a walking route, which drops down beside a fenced-off water channel. Follow the path through the trees along the shoreline until you cross a small stone slab bridge and ascend a long flight of wooden steps.

5 At the top of the steps turn left, before the wall, and follow this path as it resumes its twisting route among the waterside undergrowth with periodic views across the reservoir. Rejoin the main track and turn left to arrive at the end of the dam of the middle reservoir.

6 Go right on the main route, which swings into woodland. Ignore paths off left and right and maintain your general height and direction above the shoreline among mature beech trees. When you reach a junction of routes at the end of the lower reservoir go left, across the dam next to the wall.

7 At the far side of the dam go up some steps and veer right to the toilets and Ranger's office. Turn left on to the lane and climb back up to the car park.

> **IN THE AREA**
>
> Chesterfield is an historic town dating back to Roman times and is well worth a visit. The parish church has a curious crooked spire. One of the more credible theories for the leaning is that the Black Death killed off many of the craftsmen of the time, and those left used unseasoned timber that buckled with the weight of the leading.

> **EATING AND DRINKING**
>
> Just to the south of Linacre is Old Brampton, where the George and Dragon pub is open all day and extends a warm welcome to walkers.

Beeley Walk 19

ON BEST BEHAVIOUR IN BEELEY

Chatsworth's handsome former estate village remains a model of refinement and charm.

The influence of Chatsworth can be felt everywhere you go in Beeley. For over two centuries it was effectively an estate village belonging to the successive Dukes of Devonshire, part of the wider Chatsworth Estate that also included the villages of Edensor and Pilsley, as well as numerous farms. Latterly, many of the properties at Beeley have been sold off, but the handsome village pub has been brought back into the Duke's control in recent years. It was formerly three separate cottages, knocked together in 1747, and King Edward VII and Charles Dickens are both said to have stayed there.

Picturesque Beeley

Nearly all the buildings are constructed from a honey-coloured sandstone, giving Beeley a picturesque and harmonious feel. There has been relatively little modern development in and around the village, probably due to 250 years or so of Ducal ownership; but it also helps that the main road effectively bypasses the village, leaving the streets relatively quiet and traffic-free. Even though there are now plenty of privately owned homes, many current and former Chatsworth employees still live in Beeley.

The first part of the walk leads up through plantations to the head of Beeley Brook, then swings across fields below Beeley Moor. In these rural surroundings, it's something of a surprise to encounter the remains of industry in the woods beyond Fallinge farm. As early as the mid-1600s, a lead smelting mill had been established on the hillside, partly fuelled by coal dug from a small seam on Beeley Moor.

Hob Hurst's House

Indeed, Beeley Moor is an intriguing place, surprisingly little visited compared to the better known moors further north, or given its proximity to Chatsworth; but that doesn't mean that there's nothing to see there. If you continue beyond the plantations towards the top of Beeley Brook and out on to Harland Edge you will come to Hob Hurst's House, a Bronze Age burial mound, unusually square in shape rather than round.

Walk 19 Beeley

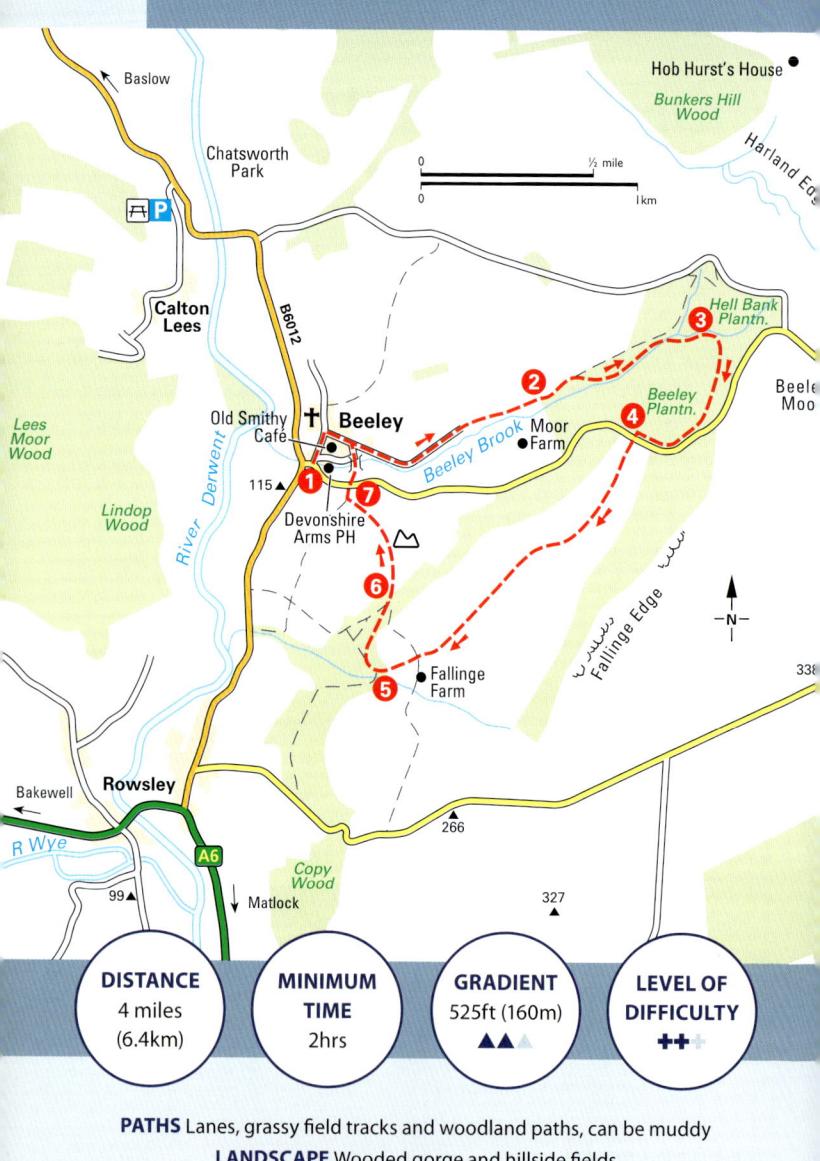

DISTANCE	MINIMUM TIME	GRADIENT	LEVEL OF DIFFICULTY
4 miles (6.4km)	2hrs	525ft (160m) ▲▲▲	++

PATHS Lanes, grassy field tracks and woodland paths, can be muddy
LANDSCAPE Wooded gorge and hillside fields
SUGGESTED MAP OS Explorer OL24 White Peak
START/FINISH Grid reference: SK 265676
DOG FRIENDLINESS Plenty of off lead potential in woods and enclosed tracks
PARKING Park responsibly in the centre of Beeley
PUBLIC TOILETS None on route, nearest at Baslow

72 40 Short Walks in the Peak District

Beeley Walk 19

WALK 19 DIRECTIONS

1 With your back to the Devonshire Arms, walk up the road opposite (Chapel Lane) past the Old Smithy café and turn right at the road junction by the village hall. Walk along the lane out of the village. It becomes unsurfaced and where it swings right, to Moor Farm, go on along the public footpath.

2 Go over the double stile and on alongside woodland on your right. After 150yds (137m) go right into the plantation at a stile/gate. Follow the level track through the plantation, crossing Beeley Brook and climbing up above the small wooded gorge.

3 Where a path joins from the left go straight on. Follow white waymarks for the concessionary footpath until eventually you climb to meet the road above. Continue along the path on the woodland edge, just below the roadside wall, for 350yds (320m).

4 Now leave the wood and cross the road for the public bridleway along the farm track opposite. Follow this for 1 mile (1.6km) until just after a large barn, fork right before Fallinge farm. Go down this track to a gate into woods.

ON THE WALK

Opposite the Devonshire Arms in Beeley are three cottages whose gables have distinctive curved sides, sometimes known as Dutch or Flemish gables. The style echoes some of the properties designed by Joseph Paxton for the Duke's nearby estate village of Edensor.

5 Follow the wide track as it curves round to the right, between the high stone supports of a long-gone bridge. Just after this, fork right for a path that eventually leads down to a squeeze stile on the edge of the woods.

6 Go into and down the field ahead, swinging left for a wall stile. Continue through several more fields, heading half left and aiming for the village below. At the bottom of a long, fenced field, turn right to reach a gate half hidden in the hedge in the bottom corner of the field.

7 Cross the road for the gated path opposite, initially heading half right then dropping sharply down to the left to cross the brook by a stone footbridge. Turn left to walk the waterside lane into Beeley.

EATING AND DRINKING

The Old Smithy in the centre of Beeley is the village shop, deli and café rolled into one, a fine establishment open daily (except Wednesday) that serves tasty snacks and main meals. There's seating inside and out and walkers are especially welcome. For more upmarket fare pop in the nearby Devonshire Arms.

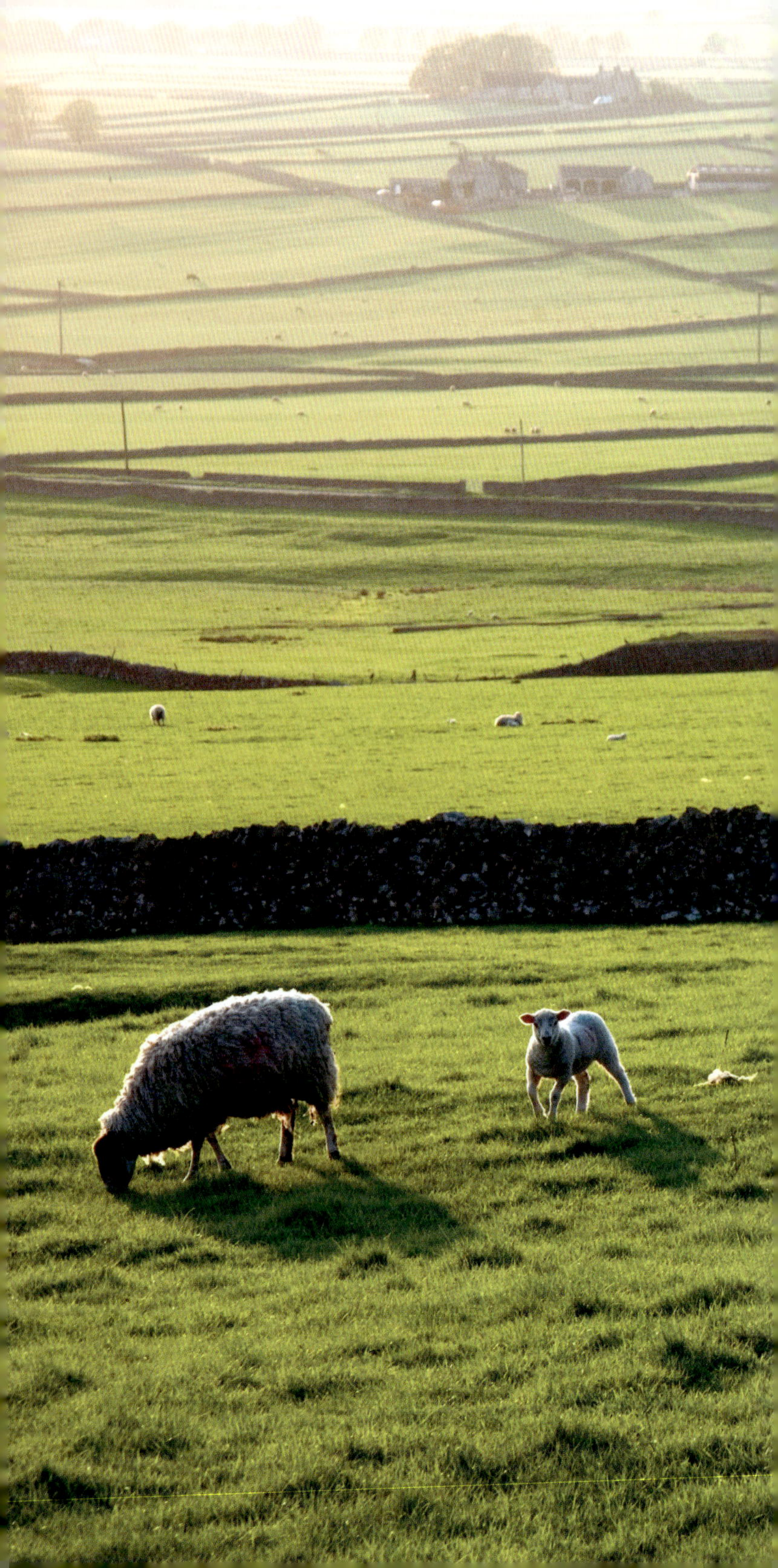

Longstone Edge

Walk 20

WIDE VISTAS FROM LONGSTONE EDGE

Enjoy sweeping views over the White Peak from a once-threatened limestone ridge near Great Longstone.

The gentle limestone scenery around the village of Great Longstone extends to the low, 3-mile (4.8km) ridge that dominates its northern horizon. Unlike the upland barriers further north and west, Longstone Edge presents a modest ripple and an inviting destination from which to look back and admire the glorious White Peak landscape, which extends for many miles.

Protected Landscape

However, in recent years Longstone Edge has been under considerable threat and battles have been fought to preserve the rock that makes this natural viewpoint. Huge chunks of the far eastern end of the hillside were eaten away by illegal quarrying, halted only after protracted legal action by the Peak District National Park Authority, supported by the local community.

Dew Ponds

Ironically, you can see virtually nothing of the quarrying from this walk on the southern side of Longstone Edge. There's far more of immediate interest on the route up from Great Longstone, along a lovely walled track called Hardrake Lane. Half-way along, over the left-hand wall, are a couple of small dew ponds (you will also pass a larger one near the entrance to Stanshill Dale towards the end of the walk). Standing water has always been scarce on the porous limestone upland of the Peak District, so in the 18th and 19th centuries small, circular artificial ponds were dug in fields to collect rainwater and snow. They would be lined with clay to make them watertight, although concrete has been used in more modern versions. Many dew ponds have disappeared, but efforts are being made to restore some of them, not least because they provide a refuge for rare wildlife like great crested newts.

Once clear of the scrub-covered hillside, this walk satisfies itself with a good viewpoint high up on the side of the edge, below the road that climbs up from Great Longstone and out of sight of the occasional quarry truck rumbling around just over the back. However, if you want to savour the view from on high then simply head up the slope a little further.

Opposite: Sheep grazing in the Peak District National Park

Walk 20 Longstone Edge

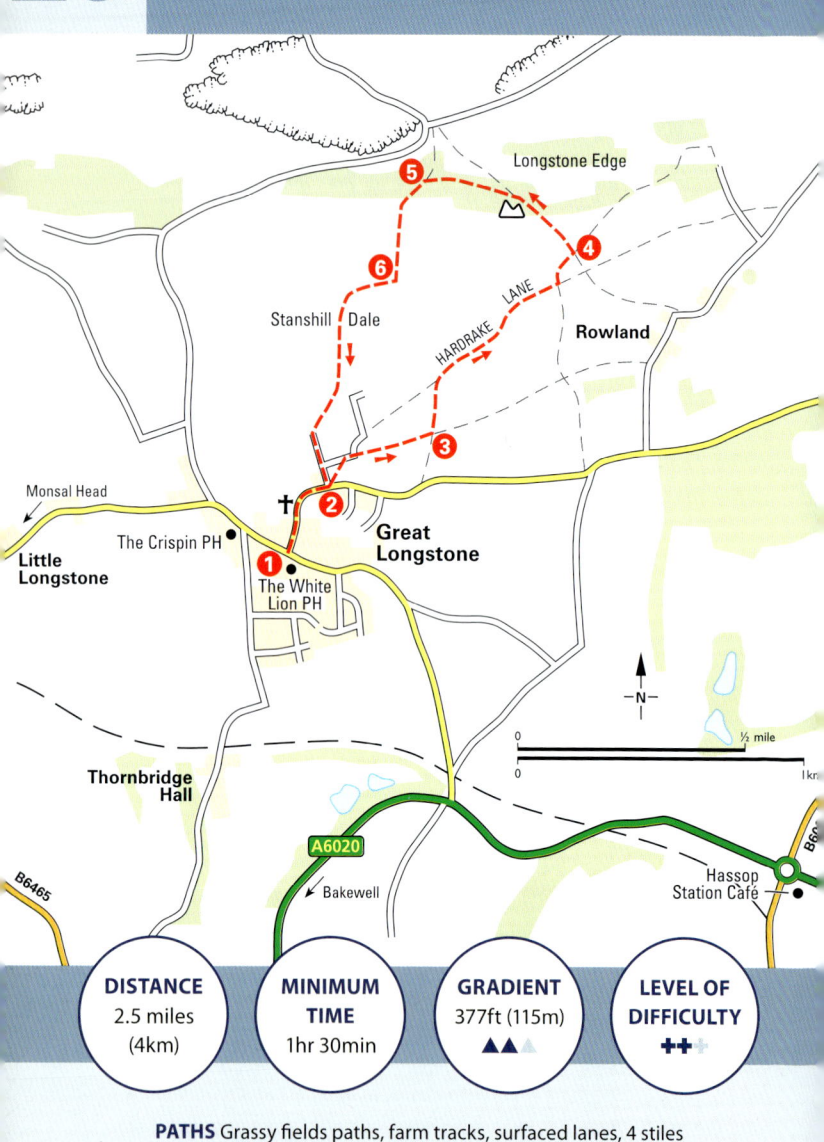

DISTANCE 2.5 miles (4km)

MINIMUM TIME 1hr 30min

GRADIENT 377ft (115m) ▲▲△

LEVEL OF DIFFICULTY ✚✚✚

PATHS Grassy fields paths, farm tracks, surfaced lanes, 4 stiles
LANDSCAPE Undulating fields of pasture and scrub-covered limestone ridge
SUGGESTED MAP OS Explorer OL24 White Peak
START/FINISH Grid reference: SK 200717
DOG FRIENDLINESS On lead around livestock but off lead on walled tracks
PARKING Street-side in Great Longstone
PUBLIC TOILETS Nearest at Monsal Head

Longstone Edge

Walk 20

WALK 20 DIRECTIONS

1 From the White Lion pub on Great Longstone's main street, walk up Church Lane opposite, taking the concessionary short-cut through the graveyard. About 150yds (137m) further on turn left into an unmade walled lane.

2 Immediately go right, through the squeeze stile in the wall, for a path slanting left across the end of the field. Turn right on to a walled path. Where this bends sharply left go straight on, through two fields, over a hard farm track, then across another field to reach a walled track at the bottom.

🍴 EATING AND DRINKING

Great Longstone's two pubs, the White Lion and The Crispin, both serve food at lunchtime and in the evening and have outdoor seating. For a café alternative head along to Hassop Station, next to the Monsal Trail, which is open daily.

3 Turn left and follow this track, called Hardrake Lane, all the way up the shallow valley until it ends. Go through the wall gap and ahead into the next field, following the waymarked route through a wooden gate. After 100yds (91m), when the wall on the left bends uphill, do likewise by going through a gate and heading up across the sloping field.

4 Beyond a wooden barrier in the fence veer half left to the top left corner of the final field. Beyond the gate the path makes its way steeply up a slope among the undergrowth and turns left on to a gentler path. Continue along this route, ignoring a public footpath off to the right, and out across the open hillside until you reach a gate.

5 Go over the stile next to the gate, then immediately left for a narrow slanting path below gorse bushes and down the hillside. At the bottom go over a stile and out across the middle of a huge field below to reach the gate on the far side.

6 Veer right into Stanshill Dale and follow the grassy path along the dale bottom. As it begins to level out make for the obvious gate in the wall above/right, then go half right through two more fields to reach the end of a long, unmade walled lane. Go down this and at the end turn right to return to the centre of the village.

🔍 IN THE AREA

If you're a beer connoisseur then don't leave the area without trying a tipple from Thornbridge Brewery. Based at nearby Thornbridge Hall, they produce a range of high quality, multi award-winning brews, of which Jaipur (a tasty IPA) is probably the best known. Visit their brewery shop in Bakewell or the Thornbridge-owned Packhorse Inn just along the road at Little Longstone.

Walk 21: Sheldon & Magpie Mine

THE LIFE OF THE LEAD MINER

The well-preserved remains of Magpie Mine are testimony to centuries of underground toil and sacrifice.

The rocks and minerals of the Peak District have always been in demand, none more so than lead. For centuries men have toiled below the surface to extract the highly valued metal, so vital for roofing and other building uses, and in its heyday (the early 1700s) as many as 10,000 miners were busy on the ore fields of the Peak District. Although profits were certainly made, many business ventures ended in failure, and abandoned shafts, redundant chimneys and grassed-over spoil tips litter the White Peak landscape. The best surviving mining remains are to be found just outside the village of Sheldon, near Bakewell.

Ancient Monument

Magpie Mine was first worked in 1740 and then more or less continuously for the next 200 years, and although now silent the buildings and even some of the machinery have been carefully preserved by the Peak District Mines Historical Society. The site, a scheduled ancient monument, shows the various stages of development, from the earliest stone buildings through to the dark, corrugated iron sheds and steel headgear that date from the last unsuccessful attempt to revive the mine in the 1950s.

A Dangerous Business

Mining was a dangerous business. There was a constant threat from rock falls and poisonous gases, as well as disputes between different miners. Magpie was just one of several mines exploiting inter-linked lead veins, which led to sometimes violent disputes. On one occasion rival miners lit fires to smoke out their competitors, resulting in the deaths of three men.

Public footpaths run across Magpie Mine and it's free to look around. What's particularly refreshing is that the site is not overrun with modern interpretation boards or waymarked trails, nor are there lots of fences or prohibitive notices – so do beware sudden drops and don't touch any of the old machinery. At weekends, there's often someone from the adjacent field centre on hand to answer questions or provide information.

Sheldon & Magpie Mine

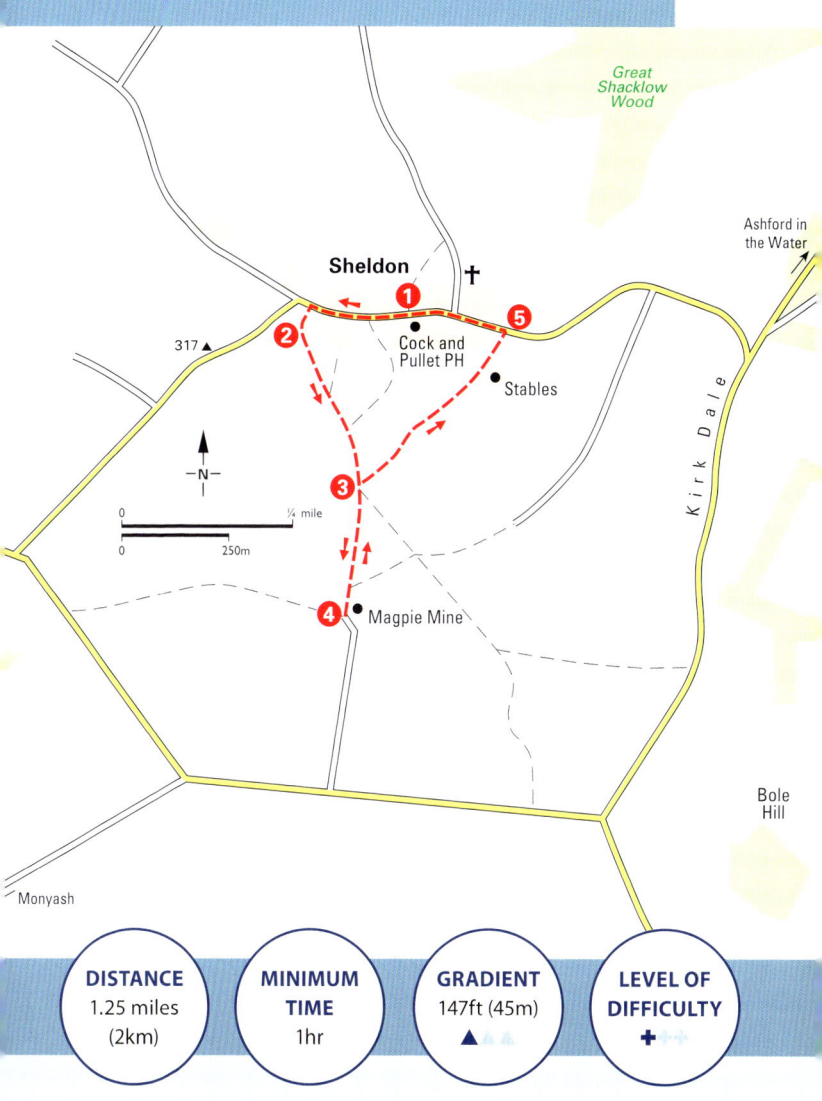

Walk 21

DISTANCE	MINIMUM TIME	GRADIENT	LEVEL OF DIFFICULTY
1.25 miles (2km)	1hr	147ft (45m)	+++

PATHS Grassy paths and tracks, 9 stiles
LANDSCAPE Gentle, open fields of limestone upland
SUGGESTED MAP OS Explorer OL24 White Peak **START/FINISH** Grid reference: SK 175687 **DOG FRIENDLINESS** Dogs on lead as cows usually graze in surrounding fields **PARKING** Roadside in centre of Sheldon
PUBLIC TOILETS None on route, nearest in Bakewell
NOTE Be careful of sudden drops and old machinery at mining site

Sheldon & Magpie Mine 79

Walk 21: Sheldon & Magpie Mine

WALK 21 DIRECTIONS

❶ Walk up the main street through Sheldon. At the top, opposite the bus stop, go left through a tiny gate just to the right of the last house, signposted 'public footpath'. Follow this to a stile then out diagonally right through a field to the far corner, with Magpie Mine in sight ahead.

❷ Go over a stile and follow the wall around to the left and through a gated opening at the end of the wall. Walk straight on and go through the gate in the wall ahead, then half right across the middle of the next field on the clear walking line. At the far side you come to another wall stile.

❸ Go over this, then fork right for a public footpath across the middle of the field towards the mine buildings, which you reach via yet another wall stile. Make your way over to the former engine house next to the tall chimney in the middle of the site.

❹ After you have inspected the whole site retrace your steps to Point ❸. Instead of crossing the field back towards the village go right, downhill and alongside the wall on your right. Go across the next field and then down through several more, keeping close to the wall on your left.

❺ When you come to some stables join an unsurfaced track which swings round to the left and down to the road. Go through the gate and walk up the road back into the centre of Sheldon.

> **IN THE AREA**
> A visit to the Old House Museum in Bakewell is highly recommended. Open April–November, it has a few mining relics, including examples of the high polished black marble that was mined at nearby Ashford, alongside a fascinating array of historical toys, textiles, tools, furniture – and even a rare Tudor toilet.

> **ON THE WALK**
> Over on the eastern edge of the Magpie Mine site, away from the stone buildings, is a replica horse gin. This wooden contraption dates from the early days of the mine and used the simple power of a harnessed horse going round and round to operate a winch up and down the shaft.

> **EATING AND DRINKING**
> Sheldon's Cock and Pullet pub (which, despite its appearance, was only built in 1995) is open all day, every day, and serves food at lunchtime and in the evening. For an excellent local café visit Monyash, just a couple of miles south-west, where the Old Smithy is a long-standing walkers' favourite and is open daily for a range of snacks and meals.

Opposite: The remains of Magpie Mine

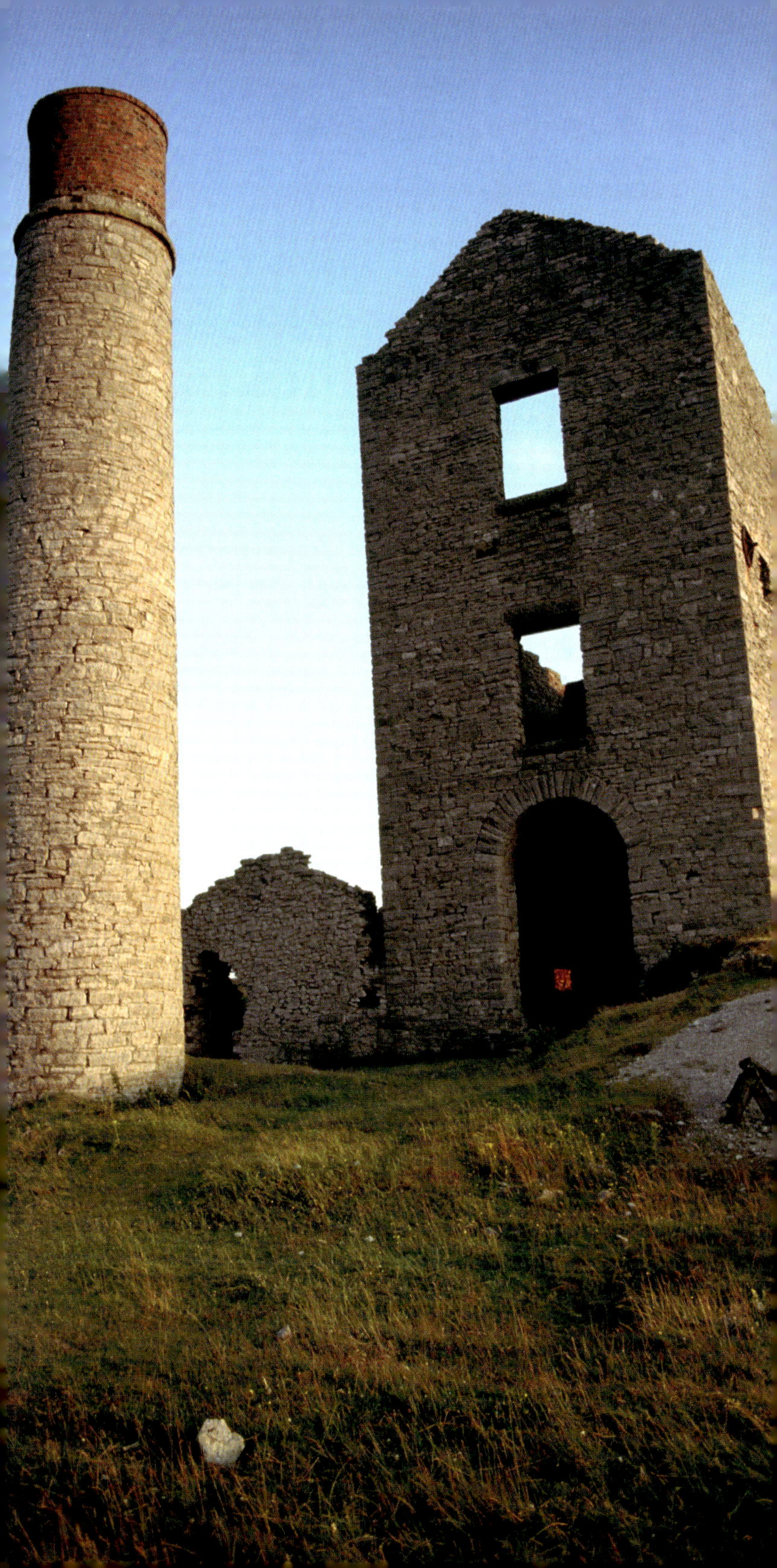

Walk 22: Chelmorton & Deep Dale

DOWN IN THE DEPTHS OF DEEP DALE

Explore a rocky dale near Chelmorton where industry and wildlife seem to co-exist.

At first glance the limestone upland of the White Peak seems quite a gentle and benign landscape, but there is a series of narrow dales etched out of the rock that can take your breath away. It's no surprise that there are several Deep Dales in the Peak District, but the one at the heart of this walk is located a mile or so west of Chelmorton and includes everything from rocky staircases to cavernous holes and huge slopes of scree.

Rocky Staircase

The route begins at the village of Chelmorton, one of the highest in the Peak District and overshadowed by the prominent hill of Chelmorton Low (1,463ft/446m), which proves a useful direction finder later on in the walk. The straightforward approach to Deep Dale across fields is no preparation for the sudden and unexpected descent into Marl Dale, a short rocky staircase taking you past the entrance to Churn Hole cave.

Marl Dale is only a short side valley that soon leads to the long and winding Deep Dale, much of it a nature reserve managed by Derbyshire Wildlife Trust. It's a dry limestone valley, with narrow slopes often edged with bare rock and cliffs or huge slopes of scree. Scrub and small patches of woodland dot the slopes, but elsewhere the rough grass sides reach down to the dale floor.

Quarry

As you turn into Deep Dale you can't help but be aware of Topley Pike Quarry. It's mostly hidden from view, but if you're there on a weekday you will certainly hear it, and as you progress into Deep Dale alongside its perimeter fence you can't help but notice the signs warning you to stay out. The opposing forces of conservation and development are close bedfellows here.

You leave the dale on a steep, winding path above a small cave. But if caves are your thing then also venture a little further up the dale to explore the much bigger Thurst House Cave. It's located high on the upper eastern slope and, when excavated in the 1880s, yielded Romano-British pottery and the bones of a Great Brown Bear.

Chelmorton & Deep Dale

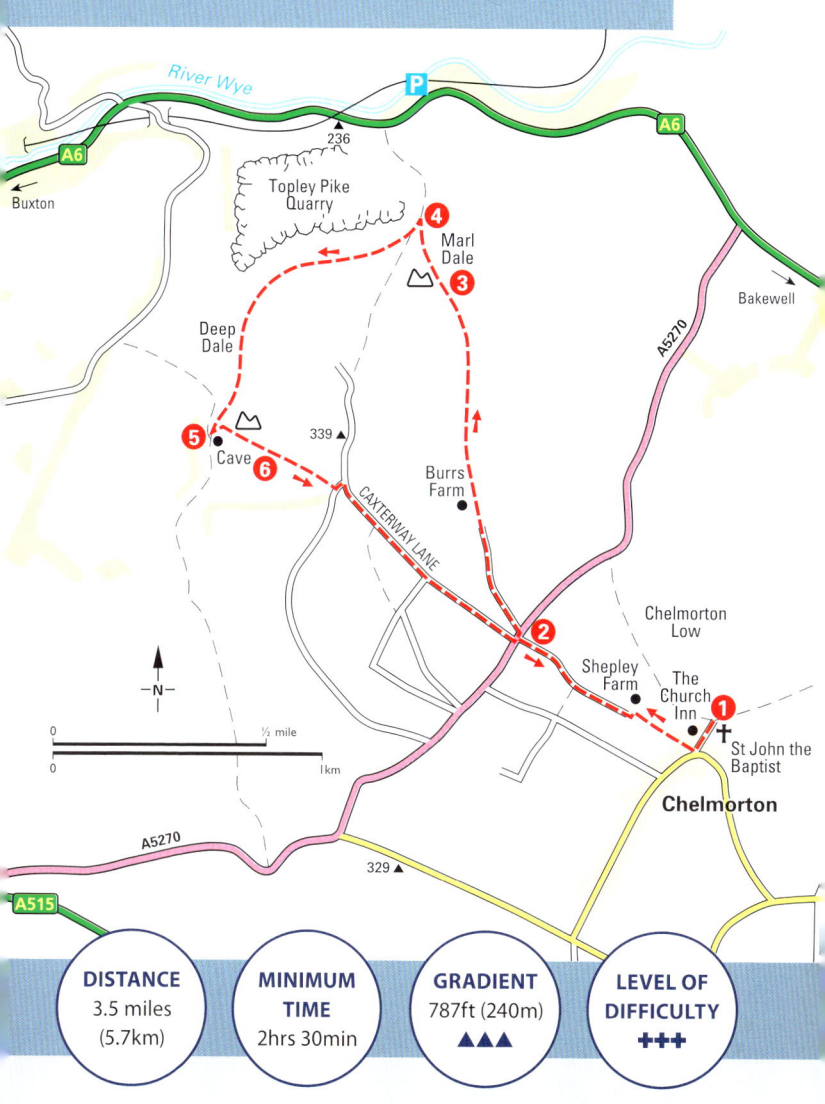

Walk 22

DISTANCE
3.5 miles (5.7km)

MINIMUM TIME
2hrs 30min

GRADIENT
787ft (240m) ▲▲▲

LEVEL OF DIFFICULTY
+++

PATHS Unmade lanes, grassy fields, rocky valley paths including steep sections, 11 stiles **LANDSCAPE** Open fields and a deep, narrow limestone dale **SUGGESTED MAP** OS Explorer OL24 White Peak **START/FINISH** Grid reference: SK 115702 **DOG FRIENDLINESS** On lead except in walled lanes away from farms **PARKING** Chelmorton village streets **PUBLIC TOILETS** None on route, nearest at Miller's Dale **NOTE** Be aware that occasional blasting takes place at the nearby quarry, Monday–Friday, 10am–6pm

Walk 22: Chelmorton & Deep Dale

WALK 22 DIRECTIONS

1 From the church or pub walk down Church Lane to the first road junction, with a bench on the corner. Turn right on a signposted public footpath and follow this between buildings away from the village. Keep left approaching Shepley Farm.

2 When you get to the road cross over and take the right-hand of two public footpaths. Follow this grassy track, initially walled then out across fields, to the right of Burrs Farm. Join an unmade farm track, then where this bends left go down to the bottom right corner and on along the foot of a shallow valley to the far end.

> ### IN THE AREA
> The Parish Church of St John the Baptist at Chelmorton is reputed to be the highest church with a spire in England, and it also has an unusual locust weather vane, reflecting the time spent by St John the Baptist in the wilderness.

3 Go over a stile and down a steep but short rocky staircase into Marl Dale. Follow the path along the valley floor and before the path swings right, into Deep Dale, look for the gate on the left.

4 Go through the gate and to the left of the Wildlife Trust noticeboard on a stepped path up the steep hillside. This swings round to the right, levels off and continues alongside the quarry's

> ### ON THE WALK
> As you walk back into Chelmorton look across to the rows of narrow fields on the right. These, and others on the other side of the one-street village, are a legacy of the medieval strip system of farming, subsequently enclosed by dry-stone walls and one of the best surviving examples of their type in the region.

boundary fence. Go down a gravel path, over a stile by a pond and out along the valley bottom.

5 After about 0.75 miles (1.2km) there's a crossroads of paths, before the dale bends left. At the junction turn left for a steep, zig-zag path up the hillside past a cave entrance. At the top go over a stile, into the field and up the right-hand edge to cross another stile.

6 Now follow the path through fields, aiming just to the right of Chelmorton Low on the skyline. When you reach a walled lane turn left, then in a few paces right on to another, called Caxterway Lane. Follow this back to the road at Point **2** and on to Chelmorton.

> ### EATING AND DRINKING
> The Church Inn at Chelmorton is a village pub, with a good selection of real ales and bar food served every lunchtime and evening. Outside is an area of patio seating, but if the village's elevation is a little chilly there's a wood burning stove indoors.

Buxton Walk 23

BUXTON'S HILLTOP TRANSFORMATION

Once an industrial wasteland, Buxton Country Park now offers woodland, a show cavern and views across the town.

Buxton Country Park is spread across the wooded hillside and open slopes of Grin Low, south of the town centre. It's a lovely place where recreation and conservation co-exist quite happily, but less than 200 years ago this land was entirely despoiled by limestone quarrying.

Grin Woods

In the 1970s the site was turned into a country park by Derbyshire County Council and its evolution has continued ever since. Buxton Civic Association, which manages Grin Woods, has produced an excellent booklet guide called Ring of Trees which describes a 10-mile (16.1km) circular walk around Buxton visiting the many individual woodlands which surround the town centre. Grin Woods is one of the largest, planted in the 1820s by the then landowner, the 6th Duke of Devonshire, after complaints that the quarry and its wasteland was becoming an eyesore. Now matured, the deciduous woodland includes beech, ash, hazel, elm and yew and the lime-rich soils of the open grassland above are also home to rare flora like orchids.

Poole's Cavern

The walk begins by skirting the old quarry, now a caravan park and campsite, then drops down through the woodland. There are numerous paths, so if you happen to be distracted by a woodpecker or squirrel and lose your way then simply aim downhill for the track along the bottom edge. Here you'll have the option of a visit to Poole's Cavern. You can join one of the regular, daily guided tours to the underground show caves, each illuminated so you can admire the impressive stalactites and stalagmites. There's also a free visitor display and café if you want to postpone a subterranean walk for another day. The final highlight of the walk is the 1,433ft (437m) open summit of Grin Low, topped by a folly called Solomon's Temple. It was built in 1896 and named after local farmer and landowner Solomon Mycock, who was responsible for an earlier structure on this spot. Its purpose was to enable the public to appreciate the view, and it still performs this function admirably.

Walk 23 | Buxton

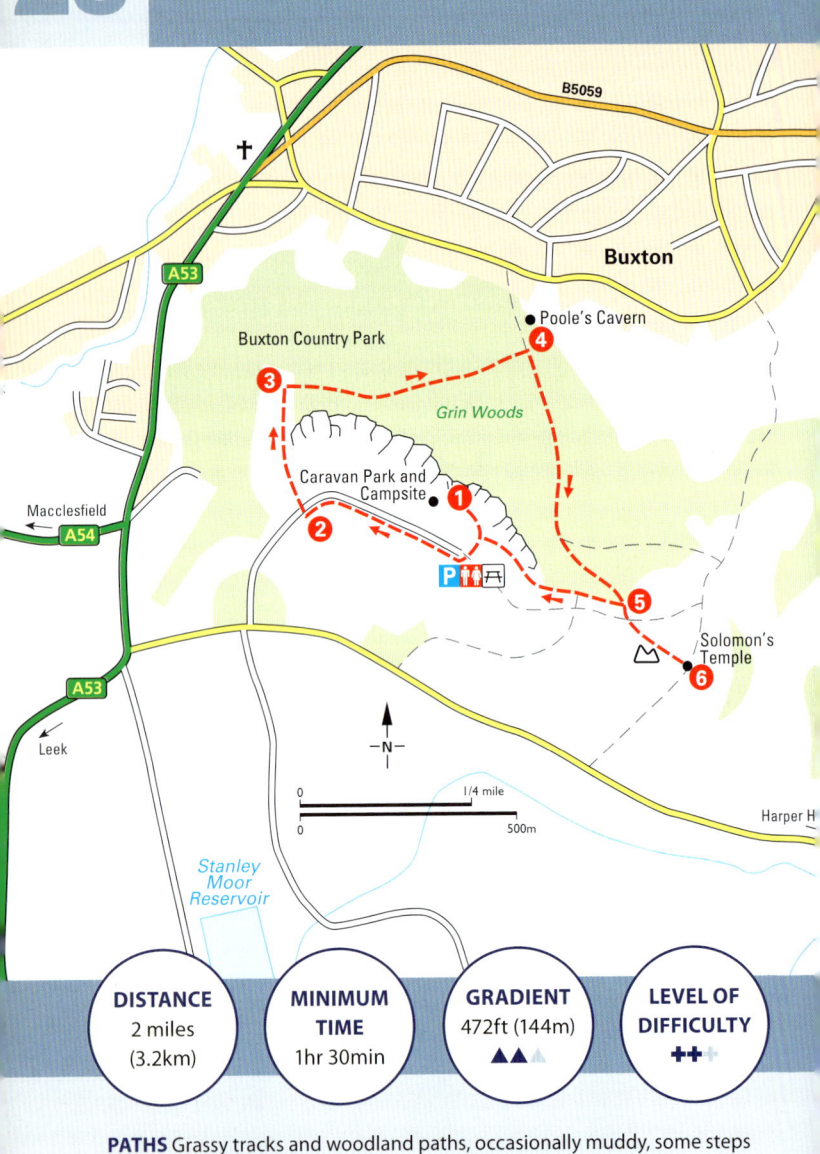

DISTANCE	MINIMUM TIME	GRADIENT	LEVEL OF DIFFICULTY
2 miles (3.2km)	1hr 30min	472ft (144m) ▲▲	++

PATHS Grassy tracks and woodland paths, occasionally muddy, some steps
LANDSCAPE Open grassy hillside, thickly wooded slopes
SUGGESTED MAP OS Explorer OL24 White Peak
START/FINISH Grid reference: SK 049718
DOG FRIENDLINESS Good off-lead route
PARKING Grin Low pay car park, locked overnight
PUBLIC TOILETS At car park

86   40 Short Walks in the Peak District

Buxton Walk 23

WALK 23 DIRECTIONS

❶ Leave the far end of the car park on a rising path signposted 'Poole's Cavern and Solomon's Temple'. Near the top turn right for a fenced path above the car park. At the very far end go through a gate and aim half right across the grassy hillside to the road.

❷ Go across the road and with the fence of the old quarry on your right continue towards the woods on the far side and down to a gate into the trees. Go through the gate and turn right.

> ### 🍴 EATING AND DRINKING
> Poole's Cavern café is open for visiting walkers when the cavern is open (most days), otherwise head into Buxton town centre for a huge choice. The Pavilion Café by the Pavilion Gardens is one of the best, featuring a large self-service café or a table service restaurant.

❸ Descend some steps into the woods, fork right, then right again after some more steps. Keep to the woodland path along the top of the slope, up some further steps, then gently downhill. When you come to a signposted junction turn left ('Poole's Cavern'), then immediately right for an occasionally stepped, twisting path down through the middle of the woods. At the bottom swing right to reach a junction.

❹ To visit Poole's Cavern, or its café, go left down the steps to the car park and visitor centre virtually in sight below. Otherwise continue along this broad, straight track, signposted 'Solomon's Temple', which rises steadily through the woodland. At a fork near the top go straight on until you reach a stile in the wall on the woodland's upper edge.

❺ Turn left and walk out across the open, bumpy hilltop to Solomon's Temple. There are paths of sorts, but it's all open and accessible and most people make their own way to the hilltop landmark.

❻ After taking in the views, return to the stile on the edge of the woods. Instead of going back over turn left for the path along the outer edge of the wall. Go up the steps at the end, through a gate, then left on the path back down to the car park.

> ### 📍 IN THE AREA
> Buxton Museum and Art Gallery on Terrace Road has fascinating exhibitions on all aspects of the Peak District's history, many of them displayed in the 'Wonders of the Peak' time tunnel. They include fossils and minerals, local social history and a fine art collection. Open Tuesday–Saturdays all year, and Sundays and Bank Holiday Mondays from Easter until the end of September (free admission).

Walk 24 — Goyt Valley

THE GOYT VALLEY OF THE GRIMSHAWES

A Manchester family's country retreat gave way to the demand for water.

In 1830, the Manchester industrialist Samuel Grimshawe chose this remote valley to build Errwood Hall, as a wedding present for his son. The family lived here 'in the style of princes'. They imported 40,000 rhododendrons and azaleas for the ornate gardens, using their own ocean yacht, the Mariquita. In its heyday the estate had a staff of 20, and included a coal mine, a watermill, housing for the servants and a private school.

The Building of the Reservoirs

But even the Grimshawes and all their accumulated wealth couldn't resist Stockport's ever-growing need for water, and in 1938 the house was demolished for the newly built Fernilee Reservoir. The dark battalions of spruce and larch, planted for a quick and plentiful supply of timber, eventually engulfed the oakwoods, and 30 years later a second reservoir, the Errwood, was built, higher up the valley. Little Goyt Bridge was dismantled and rebuilt upstream; and the valley was changed forever.

Back to the Grimshawes

This walk takes you back to the 19th century, to the time of the Grimshawes, but first you aim to get an overview of the valley by climbing the grassy spur dividing the Goyt and Shooter's Clough. After dropping into Shooter's Clough the path wanders through unruly streamside woodland to pastures and a wooded knoll. You briefly rejoin the crowds on the way to Errwood Hall. As you pass through mossy gateposts and into the grounds the order of the garden has been ruffled by nature, but the mossy foundations and floors still exist, as do some of the lower walls, arched windows and doors. You leave the hall and the crowds behind to round a wooded hill.

Uphill in a wild, partially wooded combe lies the Spanish Shrine, built by the Grimshawes in memory of their governess, Dolores de Bergrin. Inside the circular stone-built shrine there's a fine altar and colourful mosaic. If the weather is clement your spirits will be lifted by the views on the return walk along the crest of Foxlow Edge.

Goyt Valley

Walk 24

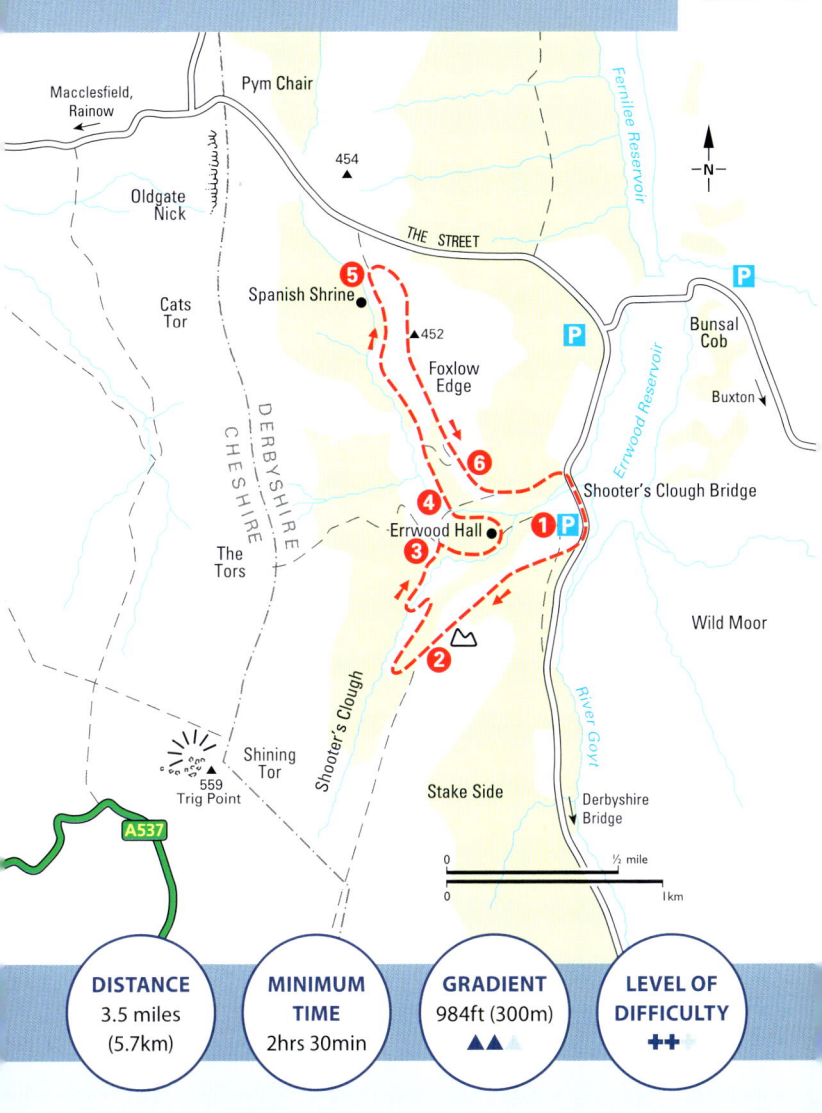

DISTANCE	MINIMUM TIME	GRADIENT	LEVEL OF DIFFICULTY
3.5 miles (5.7km)	2hrs 30min	984ft (300m) ▲▲	++

PATHS Good paths and tracks, a few stiles
LANDSCAPE Park type woodland and moor
SUGGESTED MAP OS Explorer OL24 White Peak
START/FINISH Grid reference: SK 012748
DOG FRIENDLINESS Dogs should be kept under close control
PARKING Errwood car park
PUBLIC TOILETS 1 mile (1.6km) south at Derbyshire Bridge car park

Goyt Valley 89

Walk 24: Goyt Valley

WALK 24 DIRECTIONS

❶ The path, signposted to Stakeside and Cat and Fiddle, begins from the roadside just south of the car park. Climb with it through a copse of trees, go straight across a cart track, then climb the grassy spur separating Shooter's Clough and the Goyt Valley.

❷ Go through a gate in the wall that runs along the spur and follow a path that zig-zags through the woodland of Shooter's Clough before fording a stream. The path heads north (right), through rhododendron bushes before continuing across grassland fields to a signposted junction of footpaths.

❸ Turn right here on a track skirting the near side of a wooded knoll, then ignoring the first path through gateposts, take the second left to Errwood Hall. The path continues past the ruins, before descending some steps to cross a stream via a footbridge.

❹ Climb steps on the right to reach another footpath signpost. Turn left along the path signposted 'The Shrine and Pym Chair'. This gradually swings north on hillslopes beneath Foxlow Edge. There's a short detour down and left to see the Spanish Shrine.

> **EATING AND DRINKING**
>
> There's usually an ice cream van in the car park at Errwood in summer. Try the Cat and Fiddle Inn is on the Macclesfield–Buxton road, or the Shady Oak at Fernilee (on the A5004 towards Whaley Bridge), which serves food daily.

❺ About 100yds (91m) on from the shrine the path reaches moorland. Take the path forking right, which climbs to the top of Foxlow Edge. On reaching some old quarry workings near the top, the path is joined by a tumbledown dry-stone wall. Keep to the left-hand side of the wall, except for one short stretch where the path goes the other side to avoid some crosswalls. Ignore any paths off left or right and stay with the ridge route. A wall (right) and a fence (left) soon confine the path as it descends to the woods.

❻ At a fence corner, by the woodland's edge, follow the path left, downhill through the trees where it's joined by another path. With banks of rhododendron bushes on your right, descend to the roadside at Shooter's Clough Bridge just 100yds (91m) north of the car park.

> **ON THE WALK**
>
> On the west slopes of Burbage Edge you'll see the old trackbed of the Cromford and High Peak Railway, from the tunnel near the top down to the shores of Errwood Reservoir. Although this famous railway was one of the earliest in the country, the branch through the Goyt Valley was only in use between 1852 and 1877.

90 40 Short Walks in the Peak District

Bollington Walk 25

A WALK TO WHITE NANCY ABOVE BOLLINGTON

Explore a short but scenic ridge, with a strange landmark, above the leafy town of Bollington.

Bollington lies just outside the far western edge of the Peak District National Park, but it continues to attract walkers and sightseers due in part to the short but inviting ridge of Kerridge Hill that overlooks the small Cheshire town. However it's not just the superb views that will hold your attention, but also the curiously shaped monument that occupies the far northern tip of the hill.

Striking Monument
Visible from below, and for some distance around for that matter since it stands at 920ft (280m) above sea level, White Nancy is a round stone construction that was built by the local Gaskell family in 1820 to commemorate the Battle of Waterloo. It was originally an open shelter with a stone table and benches, and was presumably a popular spot for picnics, but gradual decay and occasional vandalism led to it being bricked up, and now the building has no discernible door or windows. Nor does it bear any plaque or information panel, and most striking of all it is painted bright white. In terms of shape it resembles a large bell, or perhaps a giant chess pawn, with a large base that tapers into an odd little point. Beacons are still lit next to it to mark special occasions.

Stone Quarries
For all its scenic qualities the lower western slopes of Kerridge Hill are still quarried, although it's not visible on the walk until you reach the main summit ridge. The dressed stone is used for roofing slates and paving slabs and originally it was removed via narrow boats on the Macclesfield Canal that also served the mills and factories that once dotted the Bollington area. For a while shallow pits in the hill even yielded enough coal to supply the local engine houses, as steam power replaced water power during the Industrial Revolution's advance. But inevitably your eye will be drawn to sights further afield. If the weather is clear there will be views across Macclesfield and the Cheshire Plain to the Mersey Estuary, the urban sprawl of Greater Manchester, as well as the long, high outline of the Pennines away to the north.

Walk 25 Bollington

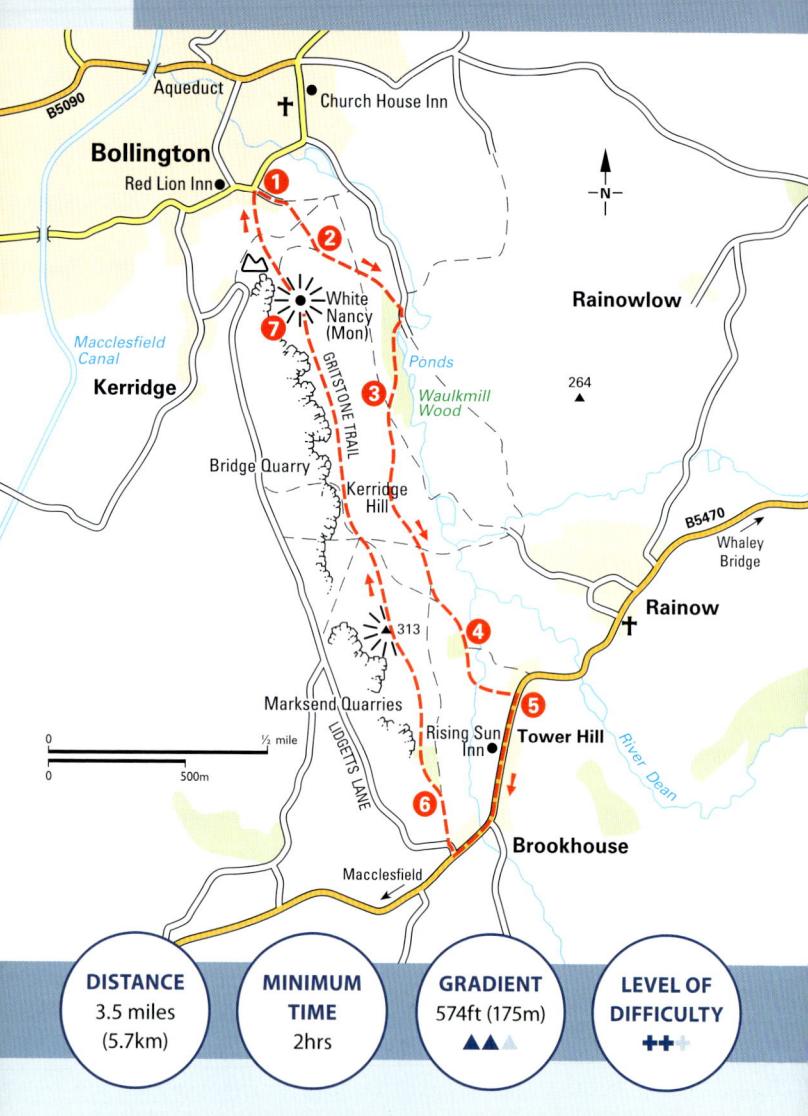

DISTANCE	MINIMUM TIME	GRADIENT	LEVEL OF DIFFICULTY
3.5 miles (5.7km)	2hrs	574ft (175m) ▲▲△	++ +

PATHS Easy field paths and farm tracks, one short, sharp descent
LANDSCAPE Mostly gentle rolling pasture and small pockets of woodland
SUGGESTED MAP OS Explorer OL24 White Peak
START/FINISH Grid reference: SJ 937775
DOG FRIENDLINESS On lead through farmland, but off lead along lanes
PARKING Kerbside parking on Church Street or Lord Street, Bollington
PUBLIC TOILETS Bollington town centre

92 40 Short Walks in the Peak District

Bollington Walk 25

WALK 25 DIRECTIONS

1 The walk starts towards the top of Lord Street (which Church Street leads into) where it turns right at the top of a steep hill. Go along Cow Lane, a cul-de-sac, and through the gate at the far end. Take the upper of two field paths, heading half right across the sloping field on the right. Aim for the gate and cattle grid at the far left top corner.

2 Turn left on to an open farm track and follow this all the way down to the lane in the bottom of the valley. Turn right, and fork right again past some terraced cottages on your right. Follow this path through the Woodland Trust's cool and shady Waulkmill Wood.

3 Leave the wood via a stile and go across the lower part of a sloping field, then in the second field aim for the buildings on the far side. Follow the gated path around to the right, and on through hillside fields.

4 In the second field, fork left for the lower path that, beyond a gate, runs along the bottom edge of a new, mixed plantation, then down a walled track through woodland to reach the main road at Tower Hill.

ON THE WALK

In the mid-1800s there were as many as 13 mills in Bollington. The last cotton mill closed in 1960, but as you may see towards the bottom of Lord Street and elsewhere some of the town's surviving mill buildings have a new lease of life as modern offices and flats.

5 Turn right along the pavement, past the Rising Sun Inn, for 0.5 mile (800m). Turn right into Lidgetts Lane, then as it bends almost immediately left go over a high stile ahead and on to a gated track past a row of hawthorn trees. Swinging left follow this grassy path up to the ridge above – ignore the lower route by the right-hand fence.

6 Follow the obvious hilltop track all the way along the spine of Kerridge Hill, ignoring tracks off left and right.

7 After admiring the views at the monument (White Nancy) at the far end, drop sharply down the pitched path beyond, with Bollington spread out below, then cross a sunken farm lane and continue down across two more steep fields to reach a stile back into Cow Lane/Lord Street.

EATING AND DRINKING

Bollington has plenty of pubs, as well as a few cafés and a bakery on the main road (B5090). But in terms of access to the walk try the Church House Inn at the bottom of Church Street and the Red Lion Inn at the top of Lord Street; and at Tower Hill (half-way along the walk) the Rising Sun Inn. All serve food lunchtime and evening.

Walk 26: Tegg's Nose

A FINE HILLTOP PROTUBERANCE

Tegg's Nose Country Park above Macclesfield provides great walking – and even better sledging.

There are some notable hills on the western side of the Peak District, not least the mini Matterhorn of Shutlingsloe and the huge moorland ridge of Shining Tor and Cats Tor, north of the Cat and Fiddle Inn. Tegg's Nose, by comparison, is significantly lower and less of a challenge, but for the people of east Cheshire it's a perennial favourite. There are routes to suit all abilities, and although this walk involves a lengthy descent and fairly long plod back up, it's neither arduous nor technically difficult.

Gritstone Quarries

The walk begins with a tour of the old gritstone quarries that litter the hilltop. For several centuries they provided building material for local roads and houses, and were used to pave many of the streets of nearby Macclesfield. The quarry closed in the 1960s, after which the county council purchased the site and turned it into a country park. Some of the old quarrying machinery has been preserved, including such fearsome-looking apparatus as a rock crusher and swing saw. There's also an electric crane that dates from around the time of the Second World War when American troops were drafted to the quarry to extract rock for new runways.

Reservoirs

At the foot of Tegg's Nose lie two small reservoirs, unremarkable in themselves but when viewed with Tegg's Nose as a backdrop it makes for an attractive scene. You'll also notice the huge scree of spoil below the summit that was created by the years of quarrying. For a long time the most common way of dislodging the rock of Tegg's Nose was by blasting, which was unpopular with locals since every now and then rock debris plunged uncontrollably down the hillside and smashed through walls and even buildings below. No such dangers today, thankfully.

If you visit Tegg's Nose in winter when it has snowed make sure to bring your toboggan. The two meadows north-west of the summit are sledging fields, with nets strung up at the bottom to stop people hitting the walls.

Tegg's Nose

Walk 26

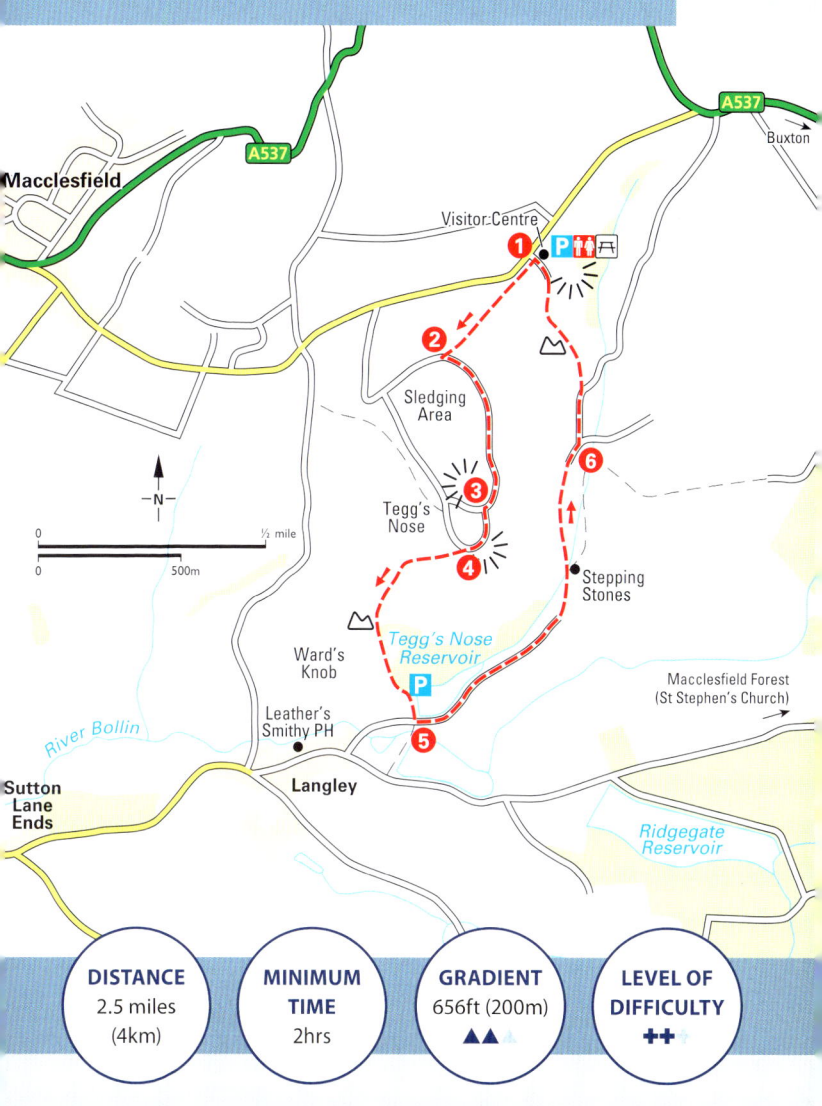

| **DISTANCE** 2.5 miles (4km) | **MINIMUM TIME** 2hrs | **GRADIENT** 656ft (200m) ▲▲ | **LEVEL OF DIFFICULTY** ++ |

PATHS Firm tracks and a long, sloping grassy path, long flight of steps
LANDSCAPE Prominent hilltop with reservoirs and gentle farmland below
SUGGESTED MAP OS Explorer OL24 White Peak
START/FINISH Grid reference: SJ 950732
DOG FRIENDLINESS Off lead on tracks, but on lead around grazing cattle
PARKING Tegg's Nose visitor centre pay car park
PUBLIC TOILETS At visitor centre

Tegg's Nose 95

Walk 26: Tegg's Nose

WALK 26 DIRECTIONS

1 From the visitor centre walk to the road and turn left on to a wide gravel track signposted 'To the Country Park'. This soon veers away from the road; at the far end go through the gate.

2 Turn left, up steps, above the remains of quarries. Go past mechanical relics and continue along this wide route until it swings right.

3 Turn left on to a smaller path that snakes its way through the heather along the edge of the hilltop. Keep going until you reach the second of two small gates in the fence on the left.

4 Go through the gate and down the hillside below, following the well-walked route initially across grass. The route keeps descending, eventually into trees and a long flight of steps until you emerge at a small car park.

5 From the car park follow the road across Tegg's Nose Reservoir dam and on the far side turn immediately left for a public bridleway along a private road. Ignoring all paths off left and right, follow this route past the reservoir and across a stream via stepping stones. Eventually you emerge on the corner of a metalled lane.

6 Go left/straight on, still uphill, and when this curves gently right after 175yds (160m) take the left turn signposted 'Saddlers Way'. Follow this long, stone-pitched walled path back up to the car park and visitor centre.

ON THE WALK
The views from the 1,144ft (349m) summit of Tegg's Nose are superb. Looking south they include Shutlingsloe, Macclesfield Forest and Croker Hill, with its distinctive telecommunications tower. To the east you gaze out over the Cheshire Plain to Jodrell Bank and Alderley Edge. Some claim that on an exceptionally clear day you can even make out Liverpool Cathedral.

EATING AND DRINKING
There's often an ice cream van at the car park on summer weekends, otherwise the Leather's Smithy pub at the village of Langley, 0.5 miles (1.6km) west of Tegg's Nose Reservoir, welcomes walkers and serves a full range of food at lunchtime and in the evening weekdays and all day at weekends.

IN THE AREA
St Stephen's Church in Macclesfield Forest, east of Tegg's Nose, is famous for its rushbearing ceremony every August, when local rushes are strewn over the church floor for a week or so. It's believed that its original purpose, many centuries back, was to keep the floor clean and dry and the rushes would be left for many months.

Three Shire Heads

Walk 27

LOOKING THREE WAYS AT ONCE

A scenic packhorse bridge in the Dane valley is where three Peak District counties meet.

The well-known location where the three counties of Cheshire, Derbyshire and Staffordshire meet is called 'Three Shire Heads' on the Ordnance Survey map. However, many people, either through design or mistake, choose to spell it differently. On this walk you'll pass a signpost erected by the Peak & Northern Footpaths Society which opts for the more logical and tautologically pleasing 'Three Shires Head'.

Packhorse Bridge

Either way, the old packhorse bridge high above the youthful River Dane and surrounded by rolling moorland is a picturesque and evocative place. Below is Panniers Pool, more evidence that this was an important junction of several historic packhorse routes. The walls of the bridge were deliberately left low to allow the laden beasts, with panniers strapped either side, to cross the river without having to unload. Trains of animals would carry raw commodities like cloth, coal and hides, led by packhorsemen known as 'jaggers' (after their hardy breed of German Jaeger ponies). Salt would be brought across from Cheshire, while lead ore and lime was carried out of the Peak District.

You approach Three Shire Heads on the eastern banks of the River Dane, when you're in Staffordshire. As you are about to step on to the bridge you're momentarily in Derbyshire, then when you reach the other side of the bridge you're in Cheshire. Three counties in a matter of strides!

Unlawful Pursuits

In recent centuries, the proximity of three county borders has been used to devious ends. Unlawful pursuits like cock-fighting and illegal bare-knuckle fights were held near the bridge, but when the police of one county turned up the participants would simply cross over the water into the other and outside police jurisdiction. Another story involves the exchange of goods for counterfeit money, which was once made by a notorious gang in the nearby village of Flash. They used a button press to make fake coins, which subsequently became known as 'Flash Money'.

Walk 27: Three Shire Heads

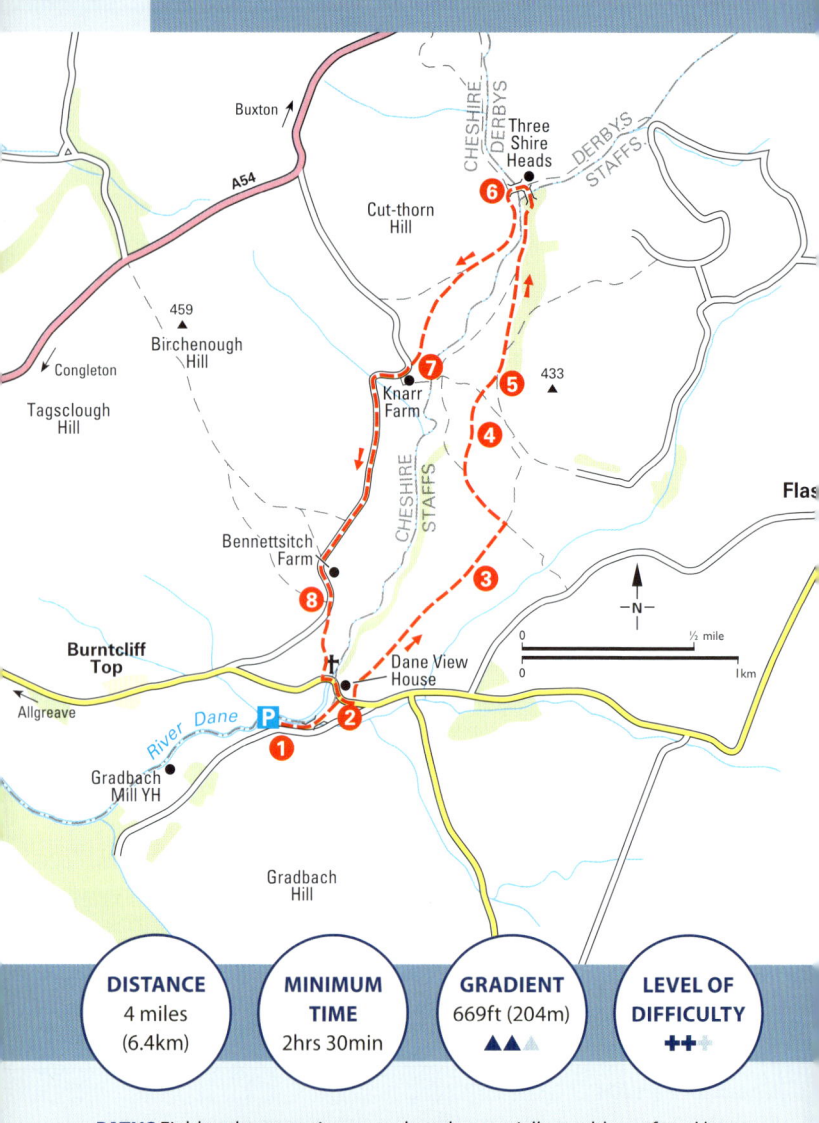

| **DISTANCE** 4 miles (6.4km) | **MINIMUM TIME** 2hrs 30min | **GRADIENT** 669ft (204m) ▲▲ | **LEVEL OF DIFFICULTY** ✚✚✚ |

PATHS Field paths, sometimes rough and potentially muddy, surfaced lanes
LANDSCAPE Rugged upland valley surrounded by moors
SUGGESTED MAP OS Explorer OL24 White Peak
START/FINISH Grid reference: SJ 998662
DOG FRIENDLINESS On lead around livestock, off lead on lanes
PARKING Gradbach car park
PUBLIC TOILETS None on route

98 40 Short Walks in the Peak District

Three Shire Heads

Walk 27

WALK 27 DIRECTIONS

1 From the far (eastern) end of the car park take the short access path parallel to the road to the footbridge across the stream. Go over this and head half right to follow the bank of the River Dane. As the road bridge comes into view go over to the gate in the wall on the right.

2 Turn right along the road, then just after the sharp bend turn left for a public footpath past Dane View House. With the buildings over to your left, go through the gate by the cattle trough and out across a succession of fields, staying close to the wall on your left.

3 After 0.5 miles (800m) the wall on your left ends. Continue straight on and after some rougher ground go left at a signpost for 'Three Shires Head'. Follow a clear grassy track through a gate and swing gradually right, across the sloping hillside. At another solitary signpost join an unmade track and continue in the same direction.

4 After 200yds (183m), and as the track dips downhill, go half right through a wall gap for a signposted public footpath slanting up across the rough pasture. Keep to the left of two hawthorn trees and continue climbing the mostly pathless hillside until you reach a footpath sign on the track above.

5 Turn left and follow this popular, walled track all the way along the narrowing valley to the packhorse bridge at Three Shire Heads.

6 Cross the bridge and turn left on a track high above the river. After 650yds (594m) go left on a path down the hillside and through a wall gate. Continue in the same direction across the open slope and at the corner of two walls fork left, aiming for the house below.

7 By an old stile turn left into the road (not the smaller driveway steeply down beside the buildings). Passing Knarr Farm on your left, follow this quiet, gated lane along the upper slopes of the valley for 1 mile (1.6km). About 150yds (137m) after Bennettsitch Farm take a signposted public footpath on the left.

8 Follow the path down beside a fence, through bracken and gorse, until after a gate and stile you reach the road at the bottom. Turn left, cross the road bridge by the chapel, then go right at the gate in the wall for the riverside route back to the car park.

> **EATING AND DRINKING**
>
> Head to the hamlet of Allgreave on the A54 Congleton–Buxton road to visit the Rose and Crown pub, which is open all day and says it welcomes dogs and muddy boots. A little further up the A54 you can enjoy some delicious home-made Hilly Billy ice cream at Blaze Farm, which also has a tea room.

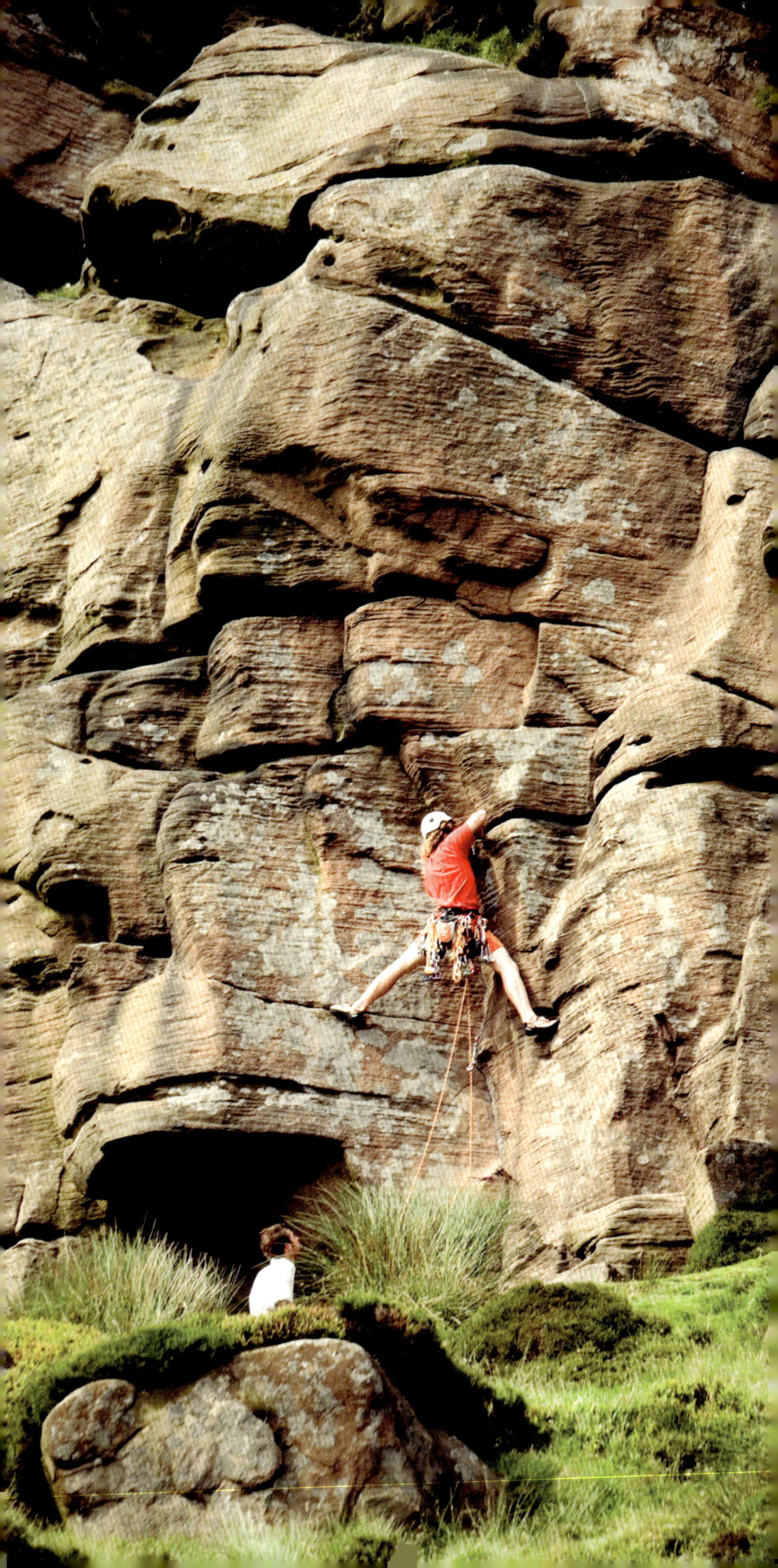

Lud's Church

Walk 28

THE RIDDLE OF LUD'S ROCKY CHASM

Follow Sir Gawain and find the secret chapel of the Green Knight.

The jagged ridge of the Roaches is one of the most popular outdoor locations in the Peak District National Park, a magnet for walkers and climbers with good paths, challenging climbs and terrific views from the top. This walk explores a quieter ridge off the northern end, but the panorama is no less splendid. To the south, below the Roaches, is Tittesworth Reservoir and distant Leek; over to the west is the distinctive jutting outline of The Cloud, near Congleton; while northwards is the equally unmistakable pointed summit of Shutlingsloe. Soon, though, you leave the open moorland top for the wooded hillside of the Dane Valley and unusual natural phenomenon.

Atmospheric Place

Lud's Church is a small chasm in the rocks, caused long ago by a landslip. It's a dark and atmospheric place, reputedly used as a hideaway and even a place of worship over the years, and inevitably associated with King Arthur.

According to the 14th-century poem 'Sir Gawain and the Green Knight', a knight on horseback gatecrashed a feast at Camelot and challenged the Knights of the Round Table. Sir Gawain rose to the challenge and beheaded the Green Knight, but the latter retrieved his head and challenged Sir Gawain to meet with him again, in a year's time, at the Green Chapel. This has been identified as Lud's Church. In the 1950s Professor Ralph Elliot identified the Roaches as the general location of the chapel.

Ghostly Gentleman

Professor Elliott's theory was supported by a group of linguists, who placed the work in the same 15-mile (24km) radius. The professor and a group of students from Keele University, where he was then based, tramped all over the countryside looking for a suitable cave to match the poetic description and Lud's Church fitted the bill. This deep cleft was created by a mass of rock slipping away from the slope of the hill. It was here that Sir Gawain kept his rendezvous with the Green Knight resulting in that ghostly gentleman losing his head for a second time.

Opposite: Intrepid rock climbers on the Roaches

Walk 28: Lud's Church

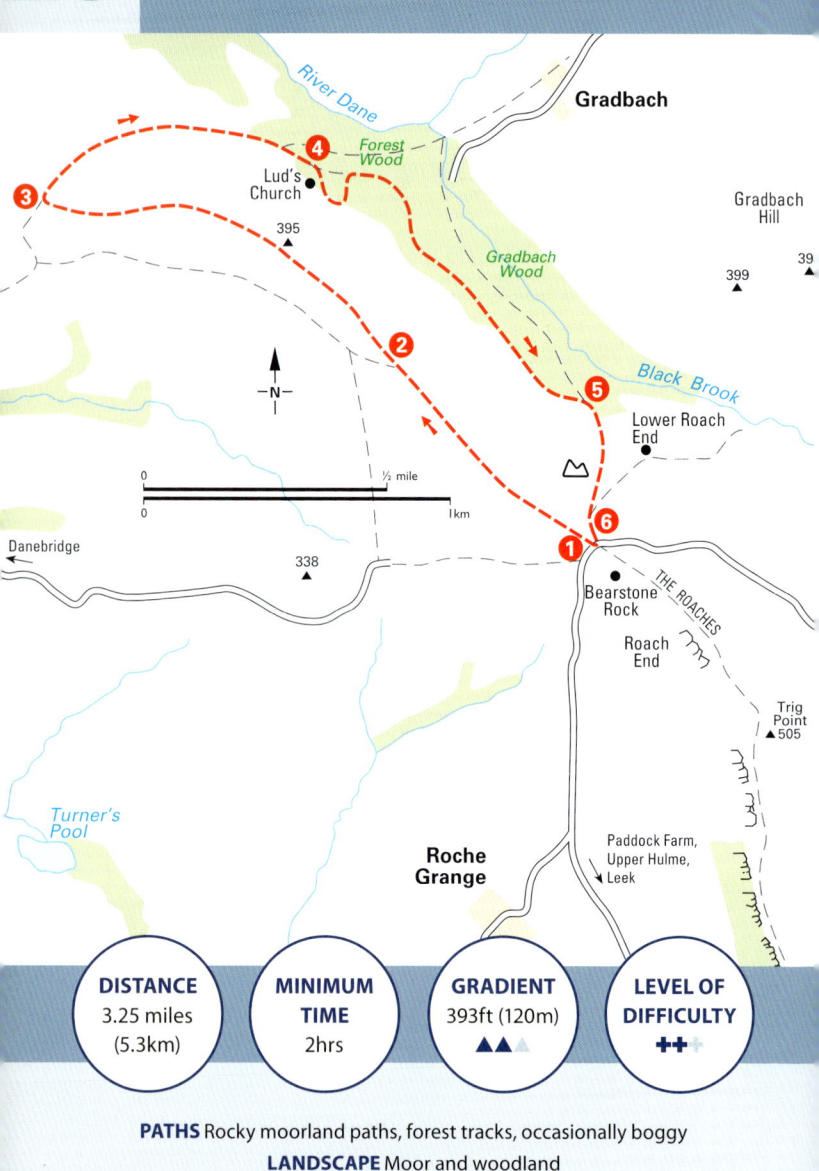

DISTANCE	MINIMUM TIME	GRADIENT	LEVEL OF DIFFICULTY
3.25 miles (5.3km)	2hrs	393ft (120m) ▲▲	++

PATHS Rocky moorland paths, forest tracks, occasionally boggy
LANDSCAPE Moor and woodland
SUGGESTED MAP OS Explorer OL24 White Peak
START/FINISH Grid reference: SJ 996644
DOG FRIENDLINESS Very good, but on lead if sheep are on the moors
PARKING Roadside parking at Roach End, near Bearstone Rock
PUBLIC TOILETS None on route, nearest at Leek

102 40 Short Walks in the Peak District

Lud's Church

Walk 28

WALK 28 DIRECTIONS

❶ Start at the bend of the road below Bearstone Rock, by the junction with the drive down to Lower Roach End. Go up the steps and through the gap in the wall signposted 'public footpath', heading north westwards. Go straight on, through a gate, for a well-walked path beside a wall along the ridge top.

❷ After 0.5 miles (800m) fork right on the concessionary path to Danebridge. Follow this path, keeping ahead at a crossroads, and through a wall gate and up to an outcrop. Carry on along the ridge, go through a gate, then head down to a signpost near a gate.

> ### 🌍 IN THE AREA
> Leek is a magnet for antiques hunters. As well as having a host of antiques dealers, there's an open-air craft and antiques market each Saturday in the historic Market Square. Other markets include the Butter Market, selling mainly fresh traditional produce, on Wednesday, Friday and Saturday.

❸ Turn right and follow the bridleway signed 'Gradbach' across the moors into the woodland. Where the route forks, in a small clearing by an outcrop, go right for a level path. Lud's Church is 275yds (251m) further on – look for the narrow fissure in the rocks on the right.

❹ After exploring Lud's Church continue along the main path from

> ### 🍴 EATING AND DRINKING
> The Roaches Tearoom at Paddock Farm sits beneath the huge rocky outcrop of Hen Cloud at the far end of The Roaches. The food is home-made, excellent and there's plenty of it. There's a conservatory overlooking a herb garden and superb views across Tittesworth Reservoir. It's open daily all year.

the entrance, or follow the path from the top of the ravine which loops back down further on. Continue for over 0.5 miles (800m) through woodland, following occasional signs for 'Roach End', until you come to a junction under a line of mature beech trees.

❺ Turn right, again signposted 'Roach End', on to a semi-paved path uphill through the thinning trees. Keep the wall on your left-hand side.

❻ Out on the moorland hillside once more and nearing the top, go through a tight squeeze stile on the left and follow the farm drive on the other side of the wall back up to the start.

> ### 🐾 ON THE WALK
> The Staffordshire Moorlands were once famous for their wallabies. Five escaped from a private zoo in 1939 and prospered so much that by the 1960s their colony had grown to over 50. After that they declined but being secretive and nocturnal animals no one is sure if they still inhabit the area.

Walk 29 Earl Sterndale & High Wheeldon

THE COMMANDING HEIGHTS OF HIGH WHEELDON

The scenic upper Dove Valley has some shapely hills with sharp slopes to match.

The River Dove is acclaimed as one of the Peak District's most scenic rivers, but while the lower end of the valley receives most of the visitors (see Walk 38) the upper reaches are, if anything, more spectacular. Instead of an enclosed wooded dale with cliffs, caves and scree, the landscape is much more open but wilder, characterised by shapely peaks with smooth grassy sides and occasional bare limestone. Parkhouse Hill and Chrome Hill are two of the most eye-catching but the huge domed lump of High Wheeldon is also worth seeking out and easier to scale. It's rather tucked away on the northern side of the valley, between Earl Sterndale and Crowdecote, but the 360-degree view from the summit is magnificent. The walk up to the very top follows well-worn footholes in the steep grassy slope. It's straightforward enough, but whatever your fitness it will make you puff.

Access Land and a Memorial

The walk begins at the village of Earl Sterndale and soon makes for the slopes of Hitter Hill and the upper lip of the Dove Valley. The hilltop is designated access land, so you can divert to the low rounded summit for the views if you wish. The route now descends to the lush valley bottom, before swinging sharply round to the foot of High Wheeldon. The sight of the hill's massive southern slopes towering above, albeit smooth and green, is rather daunting, but your route to the top approaches via the easier, northern shoulder.

It's certainly worth the effort, with the 1,384ft (422m) panorama stretching many miles. As a plaque on the summit trig point explains, High Wheeldon was presented to the National Trust in 1946 by Mr F A Holmes of Buxton as a memorial to the brave men of Derbyshire and Staffordshire who fell in the Second World War.

On the north-west side of the hill is Foxhole Cave. Its small entrance is kept locked by a sturdy iron gate, since excavations have unearthed evidence of early human activity, including neolithic implements and old animal bones, which are on display at Buxton Museum. The cave system extends for about 80ft (24m) along a series of passages and chambers.

Earl Sterndale & High Wheeldon

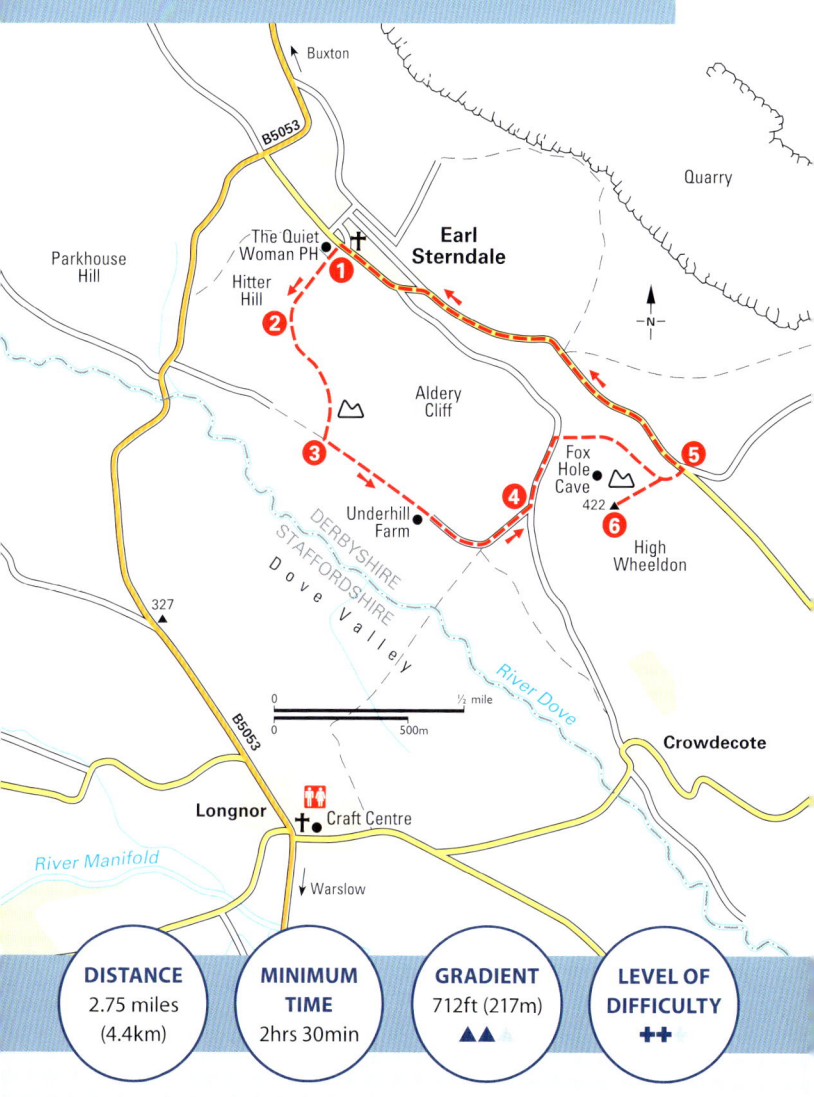

Walk 29

DISTANCE	MINIMUM TIME	GRADIENT	LEVEL OF DIFFICULTY
2.75 miles (4.4km)	2hrs 30min	712ft (217m) ▲▲	++

PATHS Field paths and tracks, steep grassy slopes liable to be slippery when wet
LANDSCAPE Narrow limestone valley of mainly pasture
SUGGESTED MAP OS Explorer OL24 White Peak
START/FINISH Grid reference: SK 090670
DOG FRIENDLINESS On lead around livestock and on National Trust land
PARKING Earl Sterndale village centre
PUBLIC TOILETS Nearest at Longnor, south on B5053

Earl Sterndale & High Wheeldon 105

Walk 29: Earl Sterndale & High Wheeldon

WALK 29 DIRECTIONS

1 From the centre of Earl Sterndale take the public footpath which passes around the right-hand side of the Quiet Woman pub. At the path junction beside the building go straight on, signposted 'Longnor and Crowdecote' and up the fields behind. Go over the stile in the top left corner and turn left on the upper slopes of Hitter Hill.

2 Keep close to the wall on your left, over another stile and alongside the wall for 100yds (91m). Look for the hawthorn tree towards the top of the slope with a blue disk attached to it, and here head half right down the steep, uneven hillside on a faint path. Go through the gated wall stile at the bottom and across a field to a building.

3 Turn left on to the track that runs past the building and follow this gated route along the top of several fields and via Underhill farmyard. Beyond this it becomes a surfaced drive and swings round to the left to join a road.

4 Turn left and walk up the road, with High Wheeldon looming above. After 330yds (302m) turn right on a public footpath opposite the former Aldery Cliff quarry, now used for climbing. Follow the path past a National Trust sign and along the foot of High Wheeldon's massive northern slopes.

5 At a second National Trust sign turn right for the steep path to the summit.

6 Retrace your steps to the (second) sign at the bottom of the slope, go through the gate and up through the field to the road above. Turn left and along the road back to Earl Sterndale.

> ### 🍴 EATING AND DRINKING
> The village of Longnor is just across the Dove valley and has plenty of choices. There are several pubs, the Longnor Craft Centre and Coffee Shop in the old Market Hall on the main square, and even a fish and chip shop with indoor seating.

> ### 🥾 ON THE WALK
> The Quiet Woman pub sign at Earl Sterndale features a headless woman. Apparently a former landlord was fed up with his wife's constant nagging, so he decided to have a quiet woman outside even if he couldn't have one in.

> ### 🔍 IN THE AREA
> Early on in the walk you will have glimpsed Parkhouse Hill and Chrome Hill further up the valley, two celebrated peaks that jut out from the valley floor like shark's teeth (they're also sometimes called the dragon's back). A well-used path traverses both tops; if you don't fancy scaling their heights after High Wheeldon they're still well worth a closer look.

Youlgreave & Bradford Dale

Walk 30

BRADFORD DALE'S PEACEFUL HIDEAWAY

Explore a dramatic valley far below Youlgreave, a village where water takes on a special meaning.

First-time visitors to Youlgreave can sometimes be seen wandering up and down the main street in search of the dale. It's not as daft as you may think, since the village sits high on the valley's northern rim with the River Bradford largely out of sight far below. Further down river, where the Bradford joins the River Lathkill at Alport, the scenery is much gentler with open fields, but this walk begins up river and immediately plunges into the deep, narrowing dale. Most of the steep slopes are clothed in mature woodland, while the river was long ago dammed to form ponds and weirs. You skirt one such weir to reach an old stone bridge at the foot of a track from Middleton.

Site of Meaning

The River Bradford enchants and inspires many people with its natural beauty and serenity, the upper section in particular providing a fleeting sense of remoteness from the outside world. At this old bridge pause a moment and inspect the stonework. Carved into it is a quote from William Wordsworth: 'Still glides the stream, and shall forever glide. The form remains, the function never dies.' It's one of 17 so-called Sites of Meaning, a Millennium project that saw local people mark the boundary of the parish of Middleton and Smerrill with inscribed sculptures or carvings carrying specially chosen text.

Clean Water

Water and the River Bradford have played a significant part in the history of Youlgreave. Once the village drew its water from the river, but in the early 1800s the women of the village successfully campaigned for a new supply of safer, cleaner drinking water, piped from a local spring and held in the odd-looking round stone tank that still adorns Youlgreave's main square. Nearly 200 years later the community-owned Youlgrave Waterworks Ltd continues to supply the village with locally sourced drinking water and is one of the very few private water companies left. The ornate stone welltaps, where the water was once piped, are now ritually celebrated by well-dressings each June, when elaborate floral displays give thanks to the supply of water.

Walk 30
Youlgreave & Bradford Dale

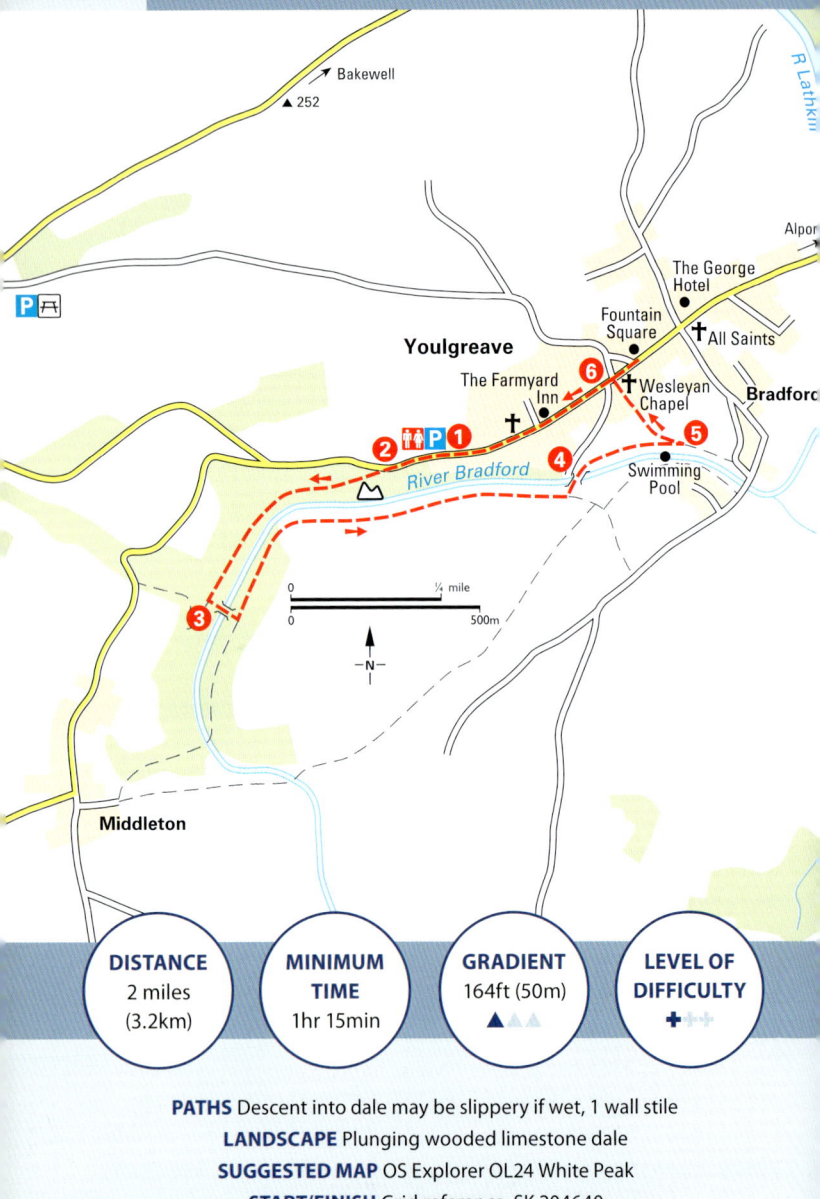

DISTANCE	MINIMUM TIME	GRADIENT	LEVEL OF DIFFICULTY
2 miles (3.2km)	1hr 15min	164ft (50m) ▲▲▲	✚✚✚

PATHS Descent into dale may be slippery if wet, 1 wall stile
LANDSCAPE Plunging wooded limestone dale
SUGGESTED MAP OS Explorer OL24 White Peak
START/FINISH Grid reference: SK 204640
DOG FRIENDLINESS Good, but keep dogs out of the river because of nesting birds
PARKING Car park at Coldwell End, Youlgreave **PUBLIC TOILETS** At car park

108   40 Short Walks in the Peak District

Youlgreave & Bradford Dale

Walk 30

WALK 30 DIRECTIONS

❶ Leave the car park and turn right to walk along the pavement away from the village for 200yds (183m), until just before you reach the first bend in the road high above the wooded dale.

❷ Go through a gate on the left for a public footpath down through dense woodland into the dale. At the bottom the path continues beside the river. Go over a wall stile and at the path junction at the end turn left. In a few paces cross an old stone bridge.

> **ON THE WALK**
>
> If you're wondering about the correct spelling of the village name you're not alone. On most road signs you'll see 'Youlgreave', and at nearby Friden even 'Youlegreave', but enter the village and you'll notice 'Youlgrave' preferred by most locals. In fact, the name has been spelt over 60 different ways since the Domesday Book, so rest easy in your confusion.

❸ Turn left and follow the wide and level riverside track downstream along the valley bottom for just under 0.75 miles (1.2km), past numerous weirs. When the path finally ends at a small metal gate go through this and over an old stone clapper bridge to cross the river.

❹ Turn immediately right and go through the squeeze stile or gate to resume the riverside route downstream, now on the left bank, as far as an artificial swimming pool where the river has been dammed.

❺ Continue for another 100yds (91m) beyond the pool and well before you get to the gate at the far end turn sharply left for a narrow but surfaced path steeply back up the grassy hillside. Continue on this through the gate at the top and up the residential road beyond. At the very top you reach a wide road junction opposite the Wesleyan Chapel.

❻ Turn right and walk 150yds (137m) to reach Fountain Square in the centre of Youlgreave, with its distinctive stone water tank or conduit head. Now about turn and walk back along Main Street, past the Old Hall and Farmyard Inn, all the the way to the car park at the far end of the village.

> **EATING AND DRINKING**
>
> The Farmyard Inn on Main Street, Youlgreave, is passed on the walk. It's open weekdays from 5pm and all day at weekends, serving a variety of hot and cold food. There's a small beer garden at the side and the pub welcomes families and dogs. For weekday lunchtime refreshment head to The George Hotel, opposite Youlgreave Church.

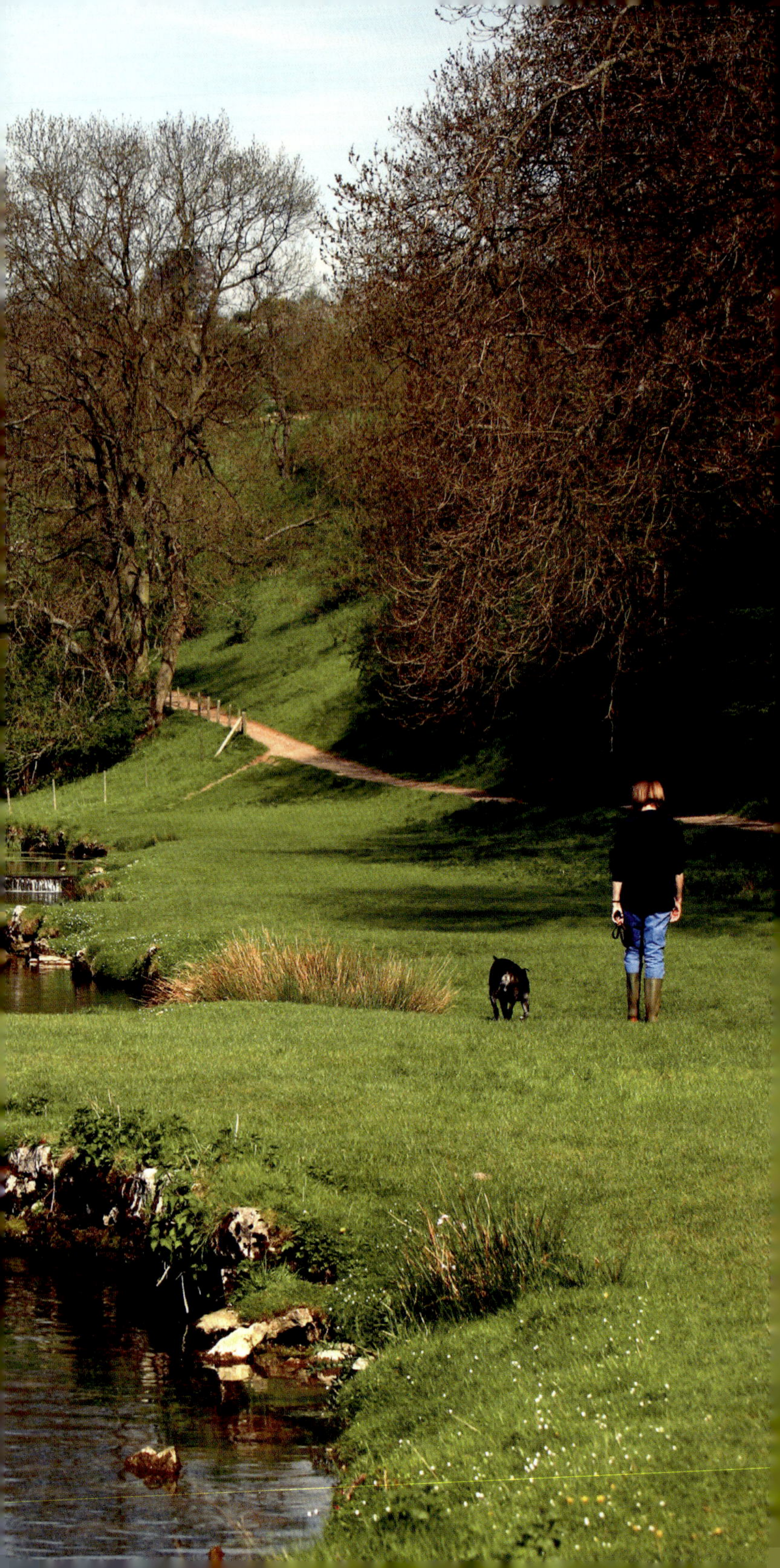

Walk 31: Lathkill Dale

LEAD MINING AND THE TRANSPARENT STREAM

Lathkill Dale contrasts the industry of long-gone lead-mining with the purity of its water.

In the 18th and 19th centuries lead miners came here and stripped the valley of its trees. They drilled and blasted shafts and adits into the white rock, built pump houses, aqueducts and waterwheels; and when the old schemes failed to realise profits they came up with new, bigger ones. Inevitably nobody made any real money, and by 1870 the price of lead had slumped from overseas competition and the pistons stopped.

Nature Reserve

On this walk you will see the fading remnants of this past, juxtaposed with the natural world, which has reclaimed the land. In reality it's Natural England which is managing the grasslands and woods as part of the Derbyshire Dales National Nature Reserve. Your route starts on a narrow winding lane from Over Haddon down to the river by Lathkill Lodge. A lush tangle of semi-aquatic plants surrounds the river and the valley sides are thick with ash and sycamore. As you make your way up Lathkill Dale you can inspect the remains of past mining efforts, beginning with an engine house built to house a giant Cornish beam engine, as well as some mossy pillars which once carried an aqueduct. A little further on are the ruins of Bateman's House, which belonged to James Bateman, agent for the Lathkill Dale Mining Company set up in 1825. It was built over a shaft dug to pump water out of the lead mine below, and today you can descend a short ladder and inspect the illuminated underground hole (wind the lever to power the light).

Conksbury Bridge

In the dry periods the river may have disappeared completely. The sun-dried soils on the southern slopes are too thin to support the humus-loving plants of the valley bottom. Instead, here you'll see the early purple orchid, cowslips with their yellowy primrose-like flowers and clumps of the yellow-flowered rock rose. However, to return to Over Haddon you head back to Lathkill Lodge and continue downstream as far as Conksbury Bridge where, unlike elsewhere on this stream, the trout pools and weirs are always full of water.

Opposite: Walking along the River Lathkill

Walk 31 Lathkill Dale

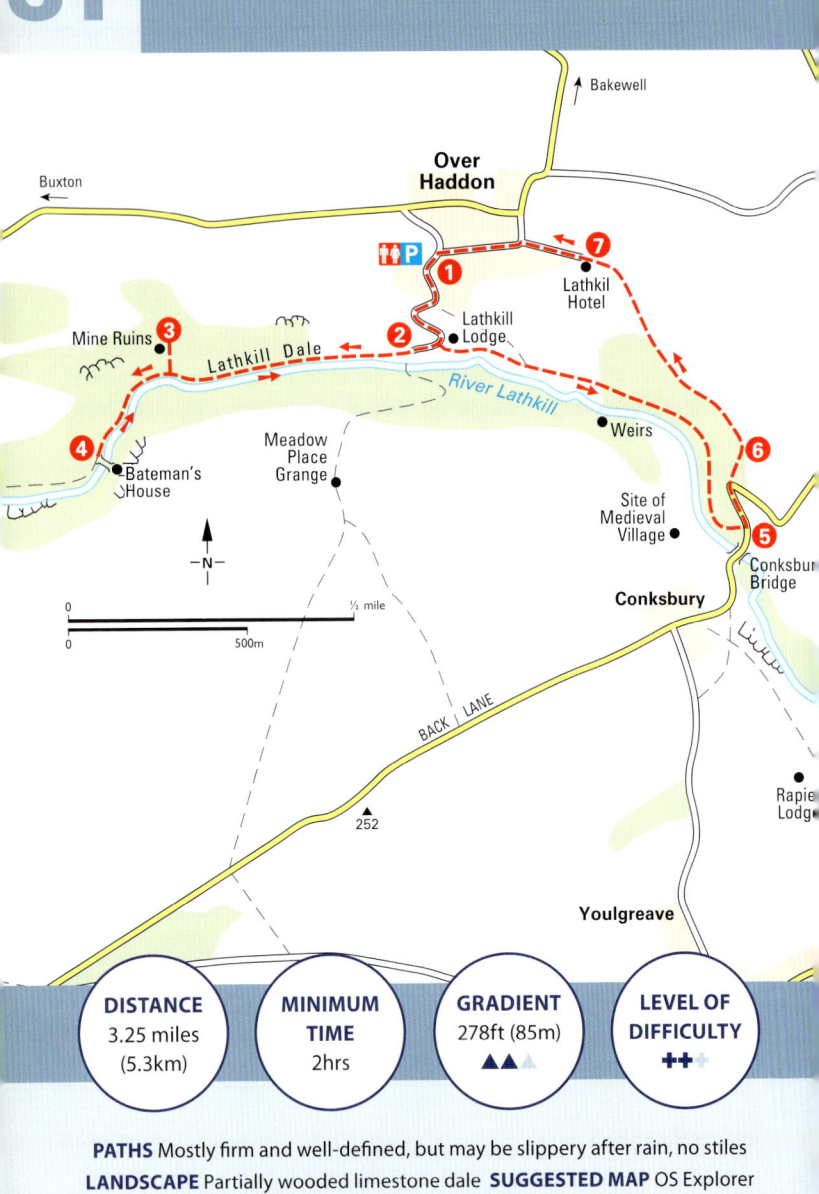

DISTANCE
3.25 miles (5.3km)

MINIMUM TIME
2hrs

GRADIENT
278ft (85m)

LEVEL OF DIFFICULTY
++

PATHS Mostly firm and well-defined, but may be slippery after rain, no stiles
LANDSCAPE Partially wooded limestone dale **SUGGESTED MAP** OS Explorer OL24 White Peak **START/FINISH** Grid reference: SK 203664
DOG FRIENDLINESS Keep dogs out of the river and on lead around livestock in fields at end
PARKING Over Haddon pay car park **PUBLIC TOILETS** At car park
NOTE Beware sudden drops at sites of old mine buildings

40 Short Walks in the Peak District

Lathkill Dale

Walk 31

WALK 31 DIRECTIONS

❶ Turn right out of the car park and right again to descend the narrow tarmac lane, which winds steeply down into Lathkill Dale.

❷ Just before reaching Lathkill Lodge at the very bottom, turn right past some stone barns along a concessionary track above the river into the National Nature Reserve. At the end of a long, open slope on your right go through some stone gateposts and turn right for a short path to the old engine house.

❸ Return to the main, dale bottom track and turn right. Continue upstream through the woods, between the former aqueduct pillars, until you reach a footbridge on the left. Go over this to visit Bateman's House.

🍴 EATING AND DRINKING

The Lathkill Hotel, at the far eastern end of Over Haddon, enjoys one of the best settings of any pub in the Peak District, with breathtaking views across the dale to Youlgreave. Bar meals are served daily, lunchtime and evening, and the pub has won several awards for its selection of real ales.

❹ Retrace your steps back down the dale all the way to Lathkill Lodge. Here go right and immediately left, before the bridge, for the surfaced path beside the garden of the house. Carry on above the river, past a series of delightful pools and weirs, until you reach Conksbury Bridge.

❺ Don't cross it but instead go left, up the steep lane to the hairpin bend. Go through the wall gap on the outside of the bend by the lay-by, then follow the very short path that curves up through the tree-covered hillside to the wall above right. Go through to the field above and turn left.

❻ With the fence on your left, make your way through the field to the gate in the wall and out along a grassy path along the upper rim of the dale, with the river far below on your left. Go through a gate in the fence on the right and continue through fields to reach Over Haddon, aiming just to the right of the white-painted Lathkil Hotel.

❼ Turn left and walk past the Lathkil Hotel along the road into the centre of the village. At a junction continue straight ahead to return to the car park.

🔍 IN THE AREA

Nearby Haddon Hall, home of the Duke of Rutland, is well worth a visit. This 14th-century country house is as impressive as Chatsworth in its own way, with beautifully laid out gardens surrounding a Gothic-style main building. See the fine medieval Banqueting Hall, and the Long Gallery, with its Renaissance panelling.

Walk 32 Stanton Moor

SACRED WORSHIP ON STANTON MOOR

A short circular walk across the mysterious Stanton Moor to discover the goings-on of ancient Druids and devilish dancers.

Stanton Moor is a small and distinctive upthrust of gritstone amid the limestone dales of the White Peak. It's moorland in miniature, where heather and silver birch provides a marked contrast to the rolling pasture and undulating river valleys all around. To the east it looks down on to the Derwent Valley and Matlock, while to the west there are panoramic views across to Bakewell and the valley of the River Wye.

Dancing on the Sabbath

There has been human activity on Stanton Moor for thousands of years. The whole of the moor is a Scheduled Ancient Monument, dotted with dozens of ancient cairns, barrows and tumuli, although much of it is hidden by heather, gorse and bilberry. Since the Bronze Age, settlers have favoured the moor for the protection that this high vantage point must have offered. However, it's an association with Druids and ritual worship that has made Stanton Moor particularly well known. Nine Ladies stone circle, situated in a clearing in the silver birch, has nine stones, which are supposed to represent women that were caught dancing on the Sabbath and turned to stone. The King Stone, set back from the circle, is the unfortunate fiddler.

Gritstone blocks and towers

On the route across the moor you will pass several giant blocks of gritstone standing isolated among the heather. Each has its own name – the Cork Stone, Heart Stone, Twopenny Loaf and the Cat Stone. They are all natural lumps of stone, weathered into fantastic shapes. Some believe that they were once probably objects of Pagan worship, although now their devotees are usually climbers who use them for practice or 'bouldering'.

As you walk along the eastern edge of the moor you'll pass what's known as the Earl Grey Tower. This folly was built by the Thornhill family, whose descendants still live at nearby Stanton Hall, to celebrate the passing of Grey's historic Reform Bill in 1832 which gave men the vote. The square stone tower (owned by the National Trust) is no longer open due to safety reasons.

Stanton Moor

Walk 32

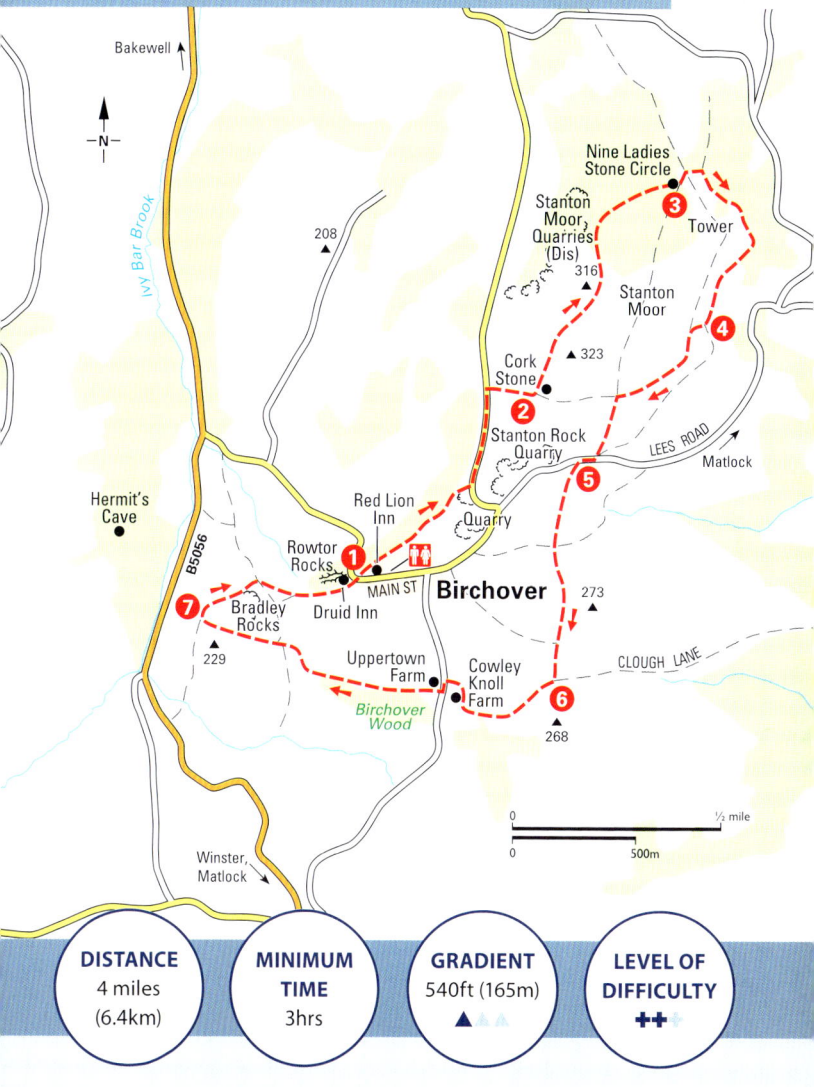

DISTANCE	MINIMUM TIME	GRADIENT	LEVEL OF DIFFICULTY
4 miles (6.4km)	3hrs	540ft (165m) ▲	++

PATHS Firm moorland tracks and field paths, a few stiles
LANDSCAPE Heather moorland and rolling pastoral landscapes
SUGGESTED MAP OS Explorer OL24 White Peak
START/FINISH Grid reference: SK 236661
DOG FRIENDLINESS On lead around livestock
PARKING Roadside parking on Main Street, Birchover
PUBLIC TOILETS Main Street, Birchover

Walk 32: Stanton Moor

WALK 32 DIRECTIONS

❶ From the Druid Inn at the end of Main Street take the signposted footpath on the bend opposite. Follow this up along a wooded ridge above the village. Where it ends at a quarry car park go left on to the road. After 0.25 miles (400m) turn right for a signposted path on to the moor.

❷ Go over a stile and veer left at the Cork Stone for a wide path across the middle of the heather moor. Stay on the main path as it enters silver birch scrub, then swing right on a wide grassy track, with a fence over to the left, until you reach Nine Ladies.

❸ Walk to the interpretation panel and turn left on the main path. In 50yds (46m) fork right for a path through the gorse and heather. Go over a stile and turn right on to a path along the high wooded edge of the moor to Earl Grey Tower. Continue on this now open path until you reach a stile on your right.

❹ Cross the stile and at the junction of tracks turn left. At a crossroads of routes turn left again, downhill, to the road. Turn right along this for 50yds (46m) and go left on a footpath.

❺ Follow this well-signposted route along the left-hand edge of a camping field, then around some buildings and ahead on a farm track along the right-hand edge of two fields. Turn right on the unsurfaced Clough Lane.

❻ Walk along the lane to its end, at Cowley Knoll Farm. Turn left on to a surfaced lane and almost immediately turn right, by Uppertown Farm, for a gated path through fields. After hugging a wall on the right the path continues past a cottage and begins a huge loop around the hilly outcrop of Bradley Rocks. At the far end go through a gate to a path junction.

❼ ignore the path downhill to the left and continue with the level track as it swings back east towards Birchover. Joining a gravel drive on a bend, take the lower route and at a crossroads of lanes go straight on past the church to return to Birchover village and Main Street.

> ### 🍴 EATING AND DRINKING
> Birchover has two good pubs. The Red Lion Inn has well-kept real ale and a varied menu served daily. The Druid Inn offers more upmarket fare and opens lunchtime and evening, and all day at weekends.

> ### ⚓ ON THE WALK
> In this area of rocky outcrops, Rowtor Rocks is certainly one of the most intriguing. You reach it up a narrow path beside the Druid Inn, and amid the jumble of huge gritstone blocks you will find rocking stones, excavated holes and caves, narrow staircases, basins and seats all carved out of the bare rock. It's a bizarre place, but watch out for some sheer drops.

Matlock & Derwent Valley

Walk 33

SCALE THE HEIGHTS ABOVE MATLOCK

A plunging gorge crossed by cable cars makes the Derwent Valley south of Matlock feel almost Alpine.

This linear walk from Matlock to Matlock Bath takes you up above the River Derwent, with views of the natural gorge. The route is perfectly safe and both the slopes and the surfaces underfoot are relatively straightforward, but do be aware that as you head towards the top there are sheer drops, in places unfenced, so children must be supervised and dogs kept on a lead.

Little Switzerland

The walk starts at Matlock's Hall Leys Park just off the town centre, heads alongside the riverside and before long you begin the ascent of High Tor, a soaring limestone crag over 300ft (91m) high and lined towards the top with sheer cliffs. You approach on what was known as the Grand Walk and look out from a summit dubbed 'Little Switzerland' by Lord Byron.

Giddy Edge

The path continues over the top of the hill, safely back from the edge; but there's another route for the seriously intrepid and the clue is in its name. The Giddy Edge path is a one-way route literally along the cliff ledges. It's not for the faint hearted and a head for heights is an absolute must.

The easy descent through lovely woodland brings you out by the cable car station, and beyond is the railway station where, if pushed for time, you could return to Matlock. But there's another, much less demanding hill to surmount, known by the collective name of the paths that criss-cross the steep wooded hillside above the river. Lovers' Walks was created as long ago as 1742 and is believed to be the earliest continuously used pleasure grounds in Britain. Routes were fashioned to visit waterfalls and selected viewpoints, as well as along the riverside below the woods. This is where your route emerges, with Matlock Bath just across the Derwent footbridge.

From Matlock Bath there are frequent daily bus and train services back to Matlock. Alternatively, if you have some puff left, there's a scenic public footpath back along the upper western slopes of the valley – see Matlock Tourist Information Centre on Crown Square for details before you set off.

Walk 33: Matlock & Derwent Valley

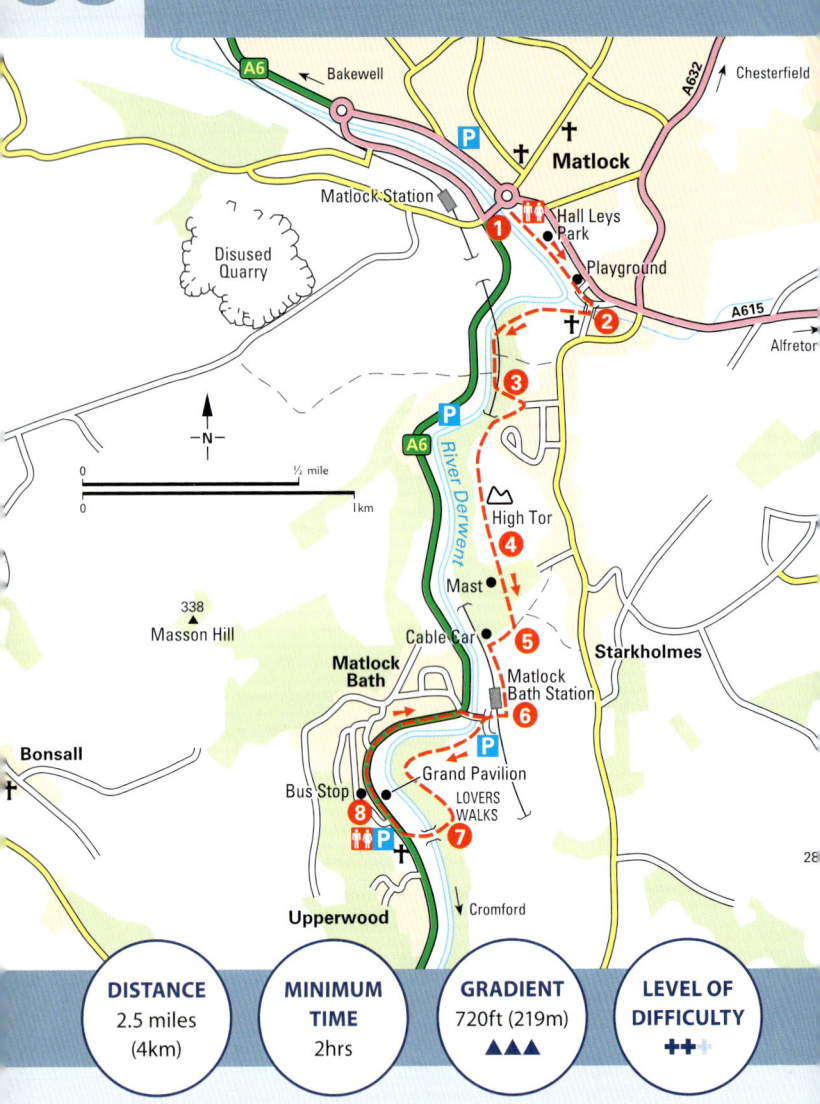

DISTANCE
2.5 miles (4km)

MINIMUM TIME
2hrs

GRADIENT
720ft (219m) ▲▲▲

LEVEL OF DIFFICULTY
++

PATHS Surfaced tracks and firm woodland paths, plenty of steps
LANDSCAPE Wooded gorge with open hilltop **SUGGESTED MAP** OS Explorer OL24 White Peak **START** Grid reference: SK 298602 **FINISH** Grid reference: SK 297585 **DOG FRIENDLINESS** On lead on streets and along cliff tops
PARKING Matlock town centre pay car park **PUBLIC TOILETS** Hall Leys Park, Matlock, and at Matlock Bath **NOTE** Beware steep and sometimes unfenced drops, so stay on the path and supervise children when necessary

118 40 Short Walks in the Peak District

Matlock & Derwent Valley

Walk 33

WALK 33 DIRECTIONS

1 From Crown Square in the centre of Matlock walk through Hall Leys Park beside the River Derwent. At the far end, next to a playground, go on to Knowleston Place for 50yds (46m), then turn right into a memorial garden.

2 Go over the footbridge, then turn right for a riverside walk below cliffs and under the railway bridge until you reach a junction. Here go left under the railway once more, not right across the footbridge over the river. Follow the path uphill until you reach houses.

EATING AND DRINKING

There's a wide choice in both Matlock and Matlock Bath, but when you end the walk at the latter try the Princess Victoria pub, on South Parade, run by the local Ashover Brewery. For café fare visit The Victorian Teashop or the Riverside Tea Rooms, both a little further along on North Parade.

3 Turn right into the grounds of High Tor. Follow the path all the way up past viewpoints to an interpretation board by a shelter. Here go right for the last few paces up to the top.

4 Take the path to the left of the Giddy Edge route and follow this over the summit and down past the transmitter mast for a stepped path past picnic tables. The route continues in zig-zags through woodland, dropping down to finally emerge by the cable car station.

5 Turn right, then before the railway bridge go left on the path signposted 'Railway Station, Lovers' Walks'. At the far end cross the railway line at the crossing by Matlock Bath station.

6 Turn left into the large car park and walk across to the coach park at the far side. Go through bollards for a rising path that swings right and up into woodland. Fork left on to a stepped path and follow this all the way along the hilltop, staying next to the fence on the left, past viewpoints, and ignoring paths downhill to the right.

7 Eventually the path turns right and descends gradually through the wooded hillside, taking a couple of zig-zags. At the bottom turn right to reach the footbridge over the river. Cross this, then turn right to walk through the gardens until you reach the Grand Pavilion on the main road.

8 The bus stop for Matlock is across the road; or turn right and walk along the wide pavement past the shops and cafés to reach the turning for the railway station.

IN THE AREA

The Peak District Mining Museum, in the Grand Pavilion at Matlock Bath, brings the industry to life with hands-on climbing shafts and hazard tunnels to crawl through, working models to puzzle over, and rocks and minerals to admire. Open daily, all year.

Walk 34 Cromford

CROMFORD AND THE HIGH PEAK TRAIL

Walk through the Industrial Revolution in a valley where history was made.

For many centuries Cromford, 'the ford by the bend in the river', was no more than a sleepy backwater. Everything changed in 1771 when Sir Richard Arkwright decided to build the world's first water-powered cotton-spinning mill here. Within 20 years he had built two more, and had constructed a new town. Cromford was awake to the Industrial Revolution and would be connected to the rest of Britain by a network of roads, railways and canals.

Cromford Mill

As you walk through the cobbled courtyard of Cromford Mill, now being restored by the Arkwright Society, you are transported back into that austere world of the 18th century, back to the times when families worked at the mills. Most of the town actually lies on the other side of the busy A6, including the mill pond which was built by Arkwright to impound the waters of Bonsall Brook, and the restored mill workers' cottages of North Street.

High Peak Trail

The next stage of the journey takes you on to the High Peak Trail, which uses the former trackbed of the Cromford and High Peak Railway, engineered by Josias Jessop and constructed in the 1830s. From its elevated position high above Cromford the line drops rapidly to the valley floor via the 0.75-mile (1.2km) long Sheep Pasture Incline. It was not unusual for wagons to career out of control on the long descent, when they could build up speeds of 120mph (193kmph). So at its foot a crash pit was built that enabled the points to be switched and the runaway truck to be diverted into a reinforced hole in the ground. You can inspect both the pit and the shattered remains of an old wagon in the centre of the trail just before you reach the bottom of the slope.

At High Peak Junction the railway met the Cromford Canal. The 33-mile (53km) canal was built in 1793, a year after Arkwright's death, to link up with the Erewash, thus completing a navigable waterway to the River Trent at Trent Lock. Today, there's an information centre here, a fascinating place to muse before the final, easy stretch along the tow path to Cromford.

Cromford Walk 34

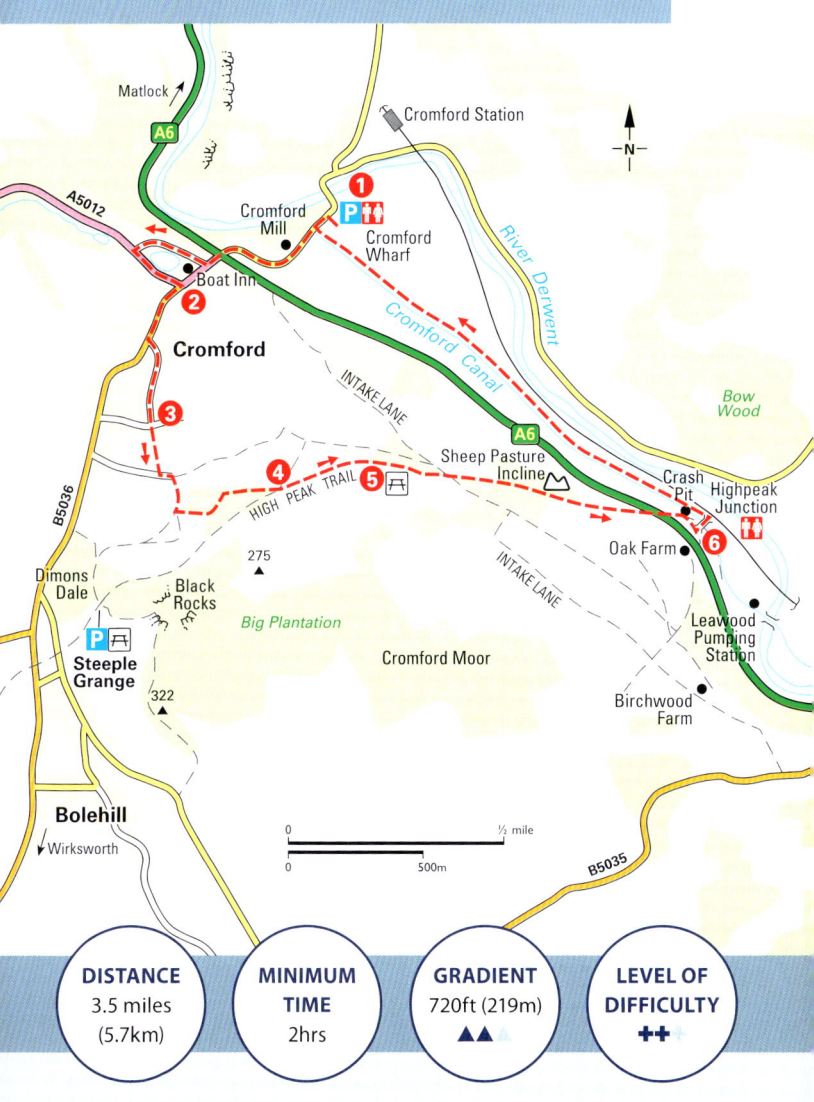

DISTANCE	MINIMUM TIME	GRADIENT	LEVEL OF DIFFICULTY
3.5 miles (5.7km)	2hrs	720ft (219m) ▲▲	++

PATHS Canal tow path, lanes, woodland path and a railway trackbed, no stiles
LANDSCAPE Town streets, wooded hillsides and valley floor
SUGGESTED MAP OS Explorer OL24 White Peak
START/FINISH Grid reference: SK 300571
DOG FRIENDLINESS Off lead on enclosed railway trail, but keep out of the canal because of wildlife **PARKING** Cromford Wharf pay car park
PUBLIC TOILETS At car park and High Peak Junction

Cromford 121

Walk 34 Cromford

WALK 34 DIRECTIONS

1 Turn left out of the car park on to Mill Road. Cross the A6 to the Market Place. Turn right along Scarthin, passing the Boat Inn and the old millpond before doubling back left along Water Lane to Cromford Hill.

2 Turn right, past the shops and the Bell Inn, then turn left up Bedehouse Lane, which turns into a narrow tarmac walkway and heads uphill past some almshouses (otherwise known as bedehouses).

3 At the top of the lane, by a street of more modern housing, go straight over for a path uphill signposted 'Black Rocks'. The footpath continues its climb to meet a lane. Turn left up the winding lane, which soon divides. Take the left fork. The tarmac lane soon becomes an unsurfaced walled track. Beyond a gate continue along a woodland path.

4 At the end don't go through the stile ahead, with open hillside beyond, but turn right to join the High Peak Trail just over the other side of the wall. Now turn left to follow the line of the former Cromford and High Peak Railway along the hilltop to the picnic tables by the former engine house at the top of the incline.

> ### 🍴 EATING AND DRINKING
> Cromford Mill has a café for drinks and light snacks. The welcoming Boat Inn free house on Scarthin, at Cromford, serves bar meals at lunchtimes and evenings and has a beer garden.

5 Walk steadily down the long, wooded slope of Sheep Pasture Incline. Continue all the way to the bottom, underneath the A6 and past the former crash pit for runaway wagons, until you emerge at High Peak Junction.

6 Cross the canal bridge and turn left before the Matlock railway to walk along the canal tow path. Follow this back to the car park at Cromford Wharf.

> ### 📍 IN THE AREA
> Cromford Mill is just one of a number of fascinating locations that make up the Derwent Valley Mills World Heritage Site. It includes Masson Mill and Smedley's Mill, at Lea Bridge, but also extends southwards to cover Belper and Derby's historic silk mills.

> ### 👣 ON THE WALK
> Try and put a few minutes by to look around the old railway workshops at High Peak Junction. If you turn right (south) along the tow path you can also visit Leawood Pumping Station, which pumped water from the River Derwent to the Cromford Canal and has been restored with a working engine.

Opposite: The Cromford Canal

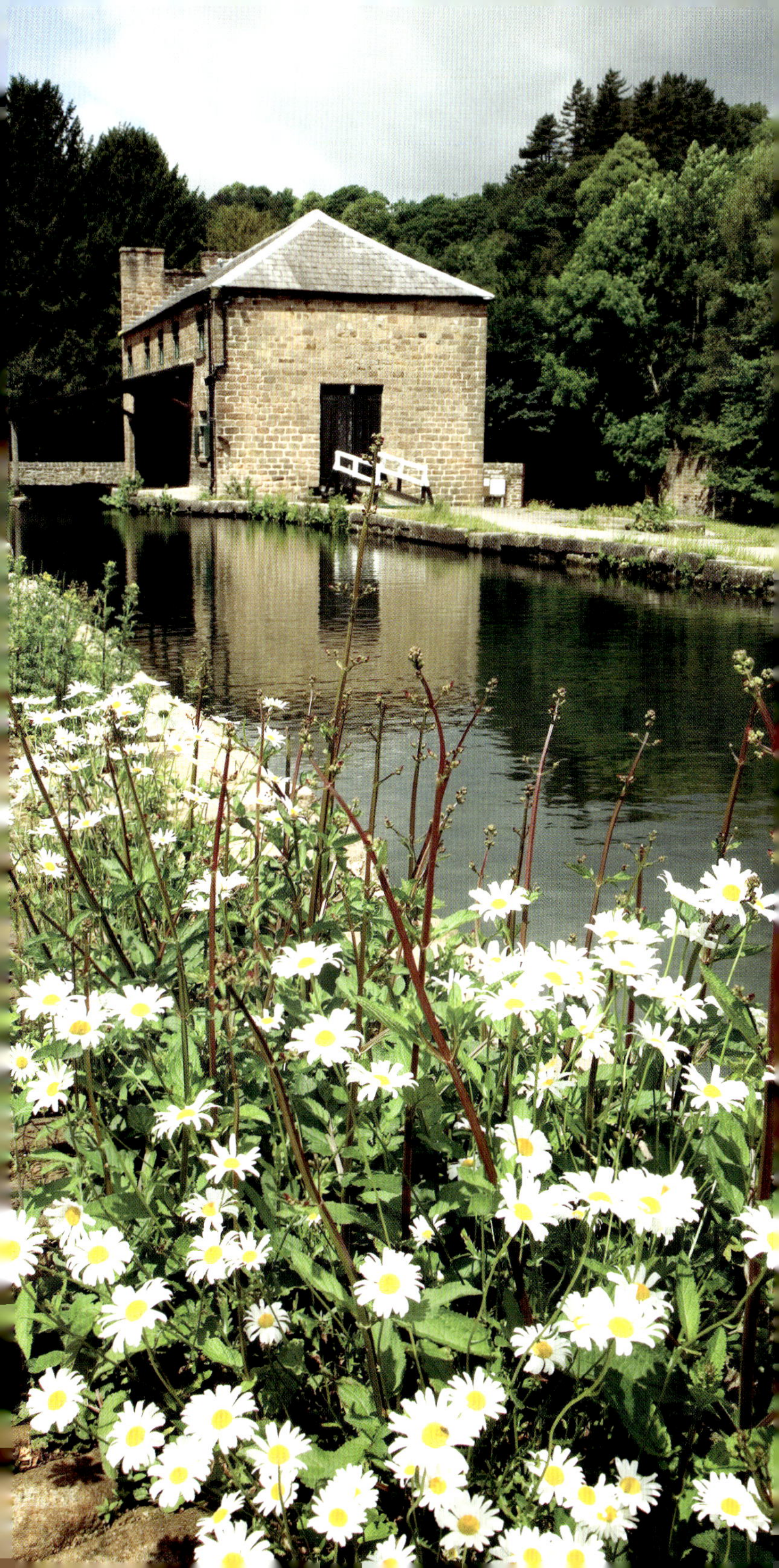

Walk 35 Wirksworth

THE TOWN AND ITS ROCK

Wirksworth's early wealth came from the ground and its legacy runs deep in the community.

This town trail begins at the Market Place in the centre of town and your first decision will be whether to visit the Heritage Centre now or at the end of the walk (open Wednesday–Saturday, April–September). Housed in a former silk mill and run by volunteers, it's a great introduction to Wirksworth.

Weaving your way through the narrow jitties (walkways), you work your way up to the top edge of town to inspect the now redundant Middlepeak Quarry, a massive hole in the hillside that for many years provided roadstone for motorways. But is was lead, not limestone, on which the town's prosperity was built. The Romans first came here in search of lead ore and in the late Middle Ages the Wirksworth 'liberty' or ore field was one of the most important in the Peak District.

Community Woodland

A little further on you come to the former Stoneycroft Quarry, now Stoney Wood Community Woodland. There are public paths, outdoor sculpture (including the wooden Peace Pole in the shape of a giant flame) and a sense that a part of Wirksworth has been returned to the community. And as you re-enter the town pause at the new orchard, where 45 Derbyshire heritage fruit trees have been planted on another part of the restored former mine.

The mining theme is continued on the eastern side of town, where you pass the historic Moot Hall. It was the seat of the miners' special Barmote Court that adjudicated specifically on mining matters. Many of the older houses in the town centre, especially on Greenhill and The Dale, were founded on the wealth of local lead merchants.

A short diversion down Coldwell Street will bring you to Wirksworth Station, home to the community-run Ecclesbourne Valley Railway which puts on events throughout the year. The walk finishes at St Mary's Church, the town's attractive parish church that rather fetchingly is surrounded by a cathedral-like close. Each September an ancient ceremony takes place when the congregation holds hands around the outside of the building. Quirky but certainly community-minded, just like Wirksworth really.

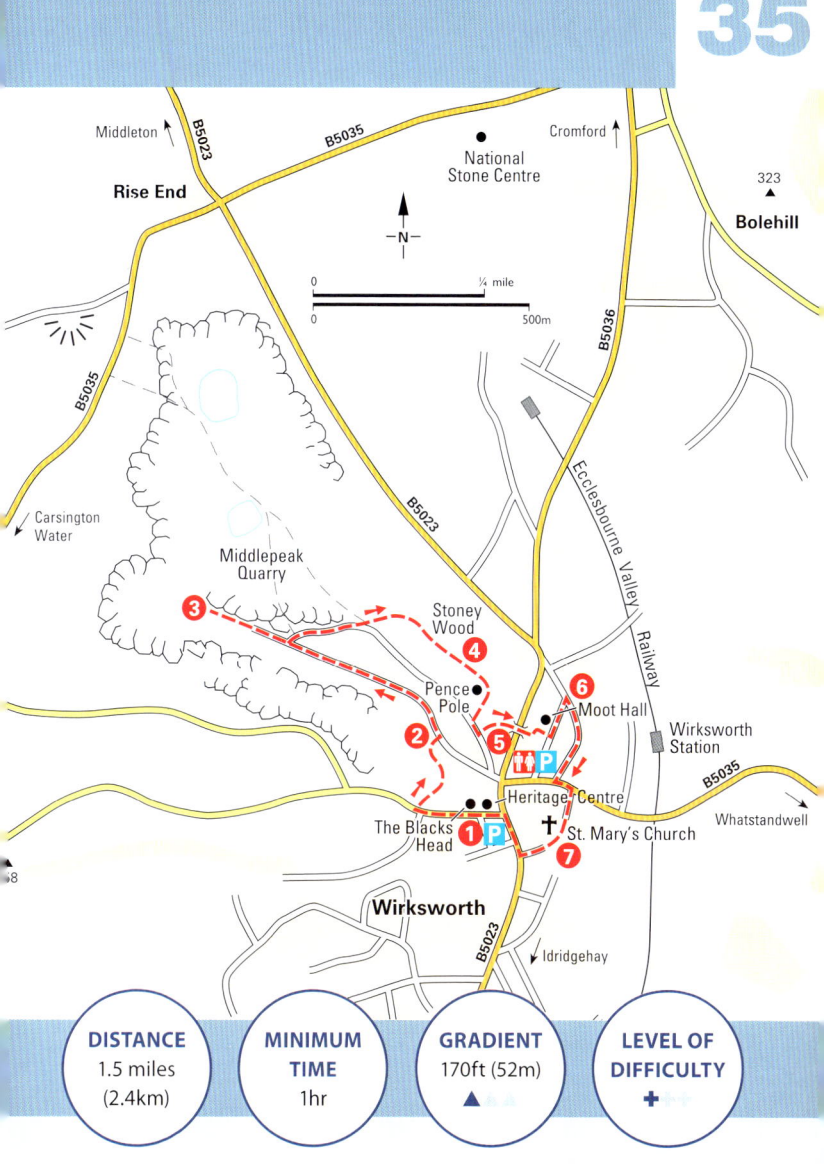

Wirksworth

Walk 35

DISTANCE	MINIMUM TIME	GRADIENT	LEVEL OF DIFFICULTY
1.5 miles (2.4km)	1hr	170ft (52m)	+

PATHS Paved paths and streets, one section of grassy slope
LANDSCAPE Town centre, plus former quarries
SUGGESTED MAP OS Explorer OL24 White Peak
START/FINISH Grid reference: SK 286539
DOG FRIENDLINESS On lead around streets
PARKING Market Place pay car park **PUBLIC TOILETS** At car park off Chapel Lane
NOTE On market day (Tuesday) park at Chapel Lane car park

Wirksworth 125

Walk 35 Wirksworth

WALK 35 DIRECTIONS

1 From Market Place, in the centre of town opposite the Heritage Centre, walk up West End past the Blacks Head pub. Turn right into Bowling Green Lane (a paved walkway between buildings), forking left twice until you drop down to reach The Dale.

2 Turn left and walk up the road, eventually leaving the houses behind, until you get to a hairpin bend. Go up the wooden steps and through the gate ahead to inspect the startling chasm of the now dormant Middlepeak Quarry.

3 Return to the road and resume your progress uphill. The road soon levels out and after 150yds (137m) go through the gap in the wall on the left and out on to the open hillside path above Stoney Wood. Follow this around to the right and down the grassy slope, with the former quarry below to your left, to reach the Peace Pole sculpture.

4 Join the gravel path from the sculpture and follow this down past a

> **EATING AND DRINKING**
> There are several good cafés and tearooms in the town centre, with Crown Yard Kitchen next door to the Heritage Centre probably the best placed. For pubs, the Blacks Head, just off Market Place, is a traditional brick-built town pub that serves food lunchtime and evenings.

small community orchard, branching right on a narrow walled path that brings you out to Greenhill, a steep road. Turn left and immediately left again for another signposted public footpath down between buildings. Go down a rough drive and at the bottom cross the footbridge above the road.

5 Follow the narrow path left then right to emerge on Chapel Lane. Turn left, past the historic Moot Hall, until you come to the junction with North End opposite the Old Lock Up (a former police station).

6 Turn right and walk all the way along North End until you reach Coldwell Street at the far end. Cross over to go along Church Street and reach the Parish Church of St Mary's.

7 Leave the church by the far (south) entrance. Turn left then immediately right to go through bollards at the end of St Mary's Gate. Follow this round to the right to reach St John's Street. Turn right to return to Market Place.

> **ON THE WALK**
> Babbington House on Greenhill is one of the oldest surviving buildings in the town (c1580s) and was built from rocks effectively quarried from the back garden. It was variously used as workhouse and cottage hospital and although now private can be admired from the road.

Minninglow

Walk 36

UNLOCKING MINNINGLOW'S MYSTERIOUS PAST

Explore a remote and enigmatic hilltop site, crowned by an ancient burial chamber.

The high and largely bare limestone landscape that ripples across much of the middle south White Peak is punctuated by a series of small, wooded crests. Of these, one of the most prominent is Minninglow, its 1,220ft (372m) hilltop topped by a clump of beech trees that is visible for miles around.

Views

Although not difficult to reach on foot, Minninglow is a surprisingly remote location. There are no main roads or villages in sight, and few modern trappings to interfere with the far-reaching views that extend in every direction. This, plus the lonely cluster of trees, contributes to a real sense of atmosphere and an away-from-it-all sort of feeling.

You can inspect the remains of a neolithic chambered cairn, built between 4500 and 2000 BC, now surrounded by a narrow strip of young trees that encircle the hilltop.

High Peak Trail

The walk approaches Minninglow along the High Peak Trail, a former railway line that from its junction with the Ashbourne–Buxton line at Parsley Hay headed east to link with the Cromford Canal in the Derwent Valley (see Walk 34). The car park at the start was a former goods yard, and after crossing a massive embankment – quite a feat of Victorian engineering in itself – the firm and easy trail reaches an old trackside quarry below Minninglow Hill. This was one of a number of limestone quarries that developed next to the line, which of course was the ideal way of transporting this valuable building commodity out of the Peak District. Today, a long-abandoned wagon sits rather forlornly by the rock face, some sleepers and even a few lengths of old rail peeping through the grass at its foot. If you look closely at the walls of the cutting you can even make out grooves drilled in the rock for the explosives.

From a neolithic burial site to a Victorian railway, this walk is a reminder that human activity has fashioned the landscape you're walking through over not just hundreds but thousands of years.

Walk 36 Minninglow

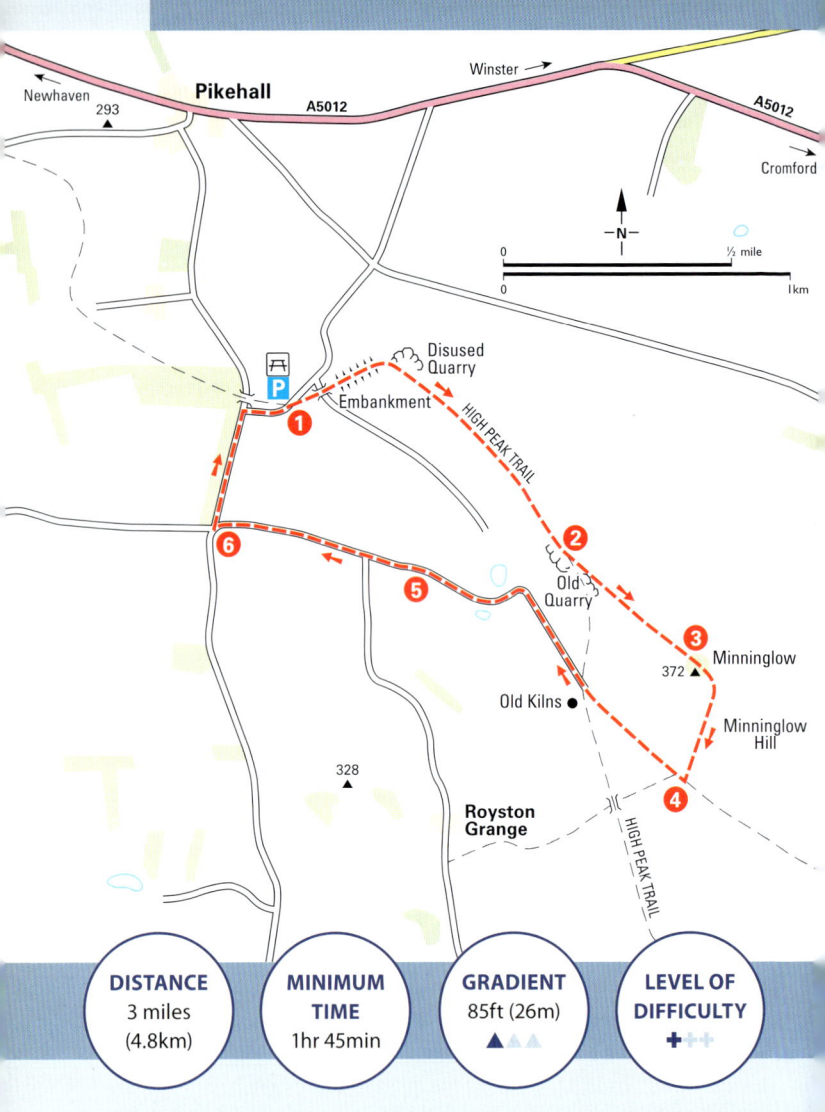

DISTANCE	MINIMUM TIME	GRADIENT	LEVEL OF DIFFICULTY
3 miles (4.8km)	1hr 45min	85ft (26m)	

PATHS Hard gravel tracks and pathless pasture **LANDSCAPE** Open, softly undulating limestone plateau **SUGGESTED MAP** OS Explorer OL24 White Peak **START/FINISH** Grid reference: SK 194581 **DOG FRIENDLINESS** Signs request dogs be kept on lead on trail and concession path to Minninglow **PARKING** High Peak Trail car park south of Pikehall **PUBLIC TOILETS** None on route, nearest at Winster or Youlgreave **NOTE** Young children should be supervised on the high, unfenced embankment at the start of the walk

128 40 Short Walks in the Peak District

Minninglow

Walk 36

WALK 36 DIRECTIONS

❶ Leave the car park on the trail heading eastwards, across the lane, signposted 'Middleton Top and High Peak Junction'. Go across a long and open embankment above the fields. Follow the trail as it swings right and beyond a small cutting reach a redundant trackside quarry.

❷ Just after the quarry, and before another high embankment, take the path on the left signposted 'Concession route to Minninglow'. Go through the gate and directly up the slope through further fields and gates to reach the tree-lined hilltop, encircled by young trees and a wall.

❸ Leave the hilltop by a gate on the opposite side from where you entered. Go out into the open field and veer right, down the gentle slope. Aim for the gate in the wall below, beyond which is a small bridge on the trail two fields away. Go through the gate and straight down the next field to the gate at the bottom.

❹ Go through the gate and turn right on to a broad, unmade walled lane. At the gated junction with the High Peak Trail go straight across, signposted 'Cycle route to Biggin', and down a long straight track into the valley. Go through a gate and follow the track left, past an old quarry and pools, then up a slope to reach a turning for a farm.

❺ Go straight ahead, along the firm farm track, until you reach a junction with a metalled lane coming up from Roystone Grange. Join this and continue in the same direction until you reach the lane at the far end.

❻ Turn right and follow the tree-lined lane as far as the trail. Turn right just before the bridge to reach the car park entrance.

> **IN THE AREA**
> About 5 miles (8km) to the north-west of Minninglow, just off the A515, is another prehistoric site that's well worth visiting. Arbor Low is a huge, rounded henge dating from around 2500 BC, with a circle of stones that all now lie flat. Like Minninglow, it sits on a prominent hilltop and its original purpose remains a complete mystery.

> **EATING AND DRINKING**
> The Miners' Standard at nearby Winster (north-east on the B5056) is a popular freehouse open every lunchtime and evening for food and drink. There's a main bar, dining room and cosy snug, with plenty of room for families and well-behaved dogs. The pub is named after the traditional rectangular dish used by local miners to measure lead ore.

Walk 37 Tissington

ON THE TRAIL OF IDYLLIC TISSINGTON

Follow the trackbed of a former railway to explore this exquisite estate village.

On this walk you save Tissington village for last, preferring instead to take to the Tissington Trail, the trackbed of the former Ashbourne–Buxton railway which was closed by Dr Beeching in 1963.

The picnic area at the start of the walk, beyond the car park fencing, is bordered by one of the original platforms of Tissington Station, and other relics dotted along the long-gone line include railway signs and signals. At Hartington, 8 miles (12.9km) further north along the trail, there's even a preserved signal box. Although the railway served one or two local quarries and there was even a daily service taking local milk to London, the railway enjoyed its heyday in the 1930s with regular excursions for ramblers visiting Dovedale and other White Peak walking destinations. For a short while there was also a through service from London Euston to Manchester.

Well Dressing

Once clear of Tissington, there are glorious views from the trail eastwards across the valley of Bletch Brook towards Bradbourne and Parwich. But soon it's back across the fields and into the estate village for a clockwise loop past the Methodist Chapel to the Coffin Well. Every year on Ascension Day Tissington's locals dress these wells. This involves making a clay-covered dressing frame on to which pictures are traced. Flower petals are then pressed into the clay, creating the elaborate patterns and pictures you see. The ceremony is unique to Derbyshire and the Peak District. Originally a pagan ceremony to appease the gods into keeping pure water flowing, it was later adopted by the Christian religion. During the Black Death, when people from neighbouring villages were being ravaged by the plague, the Tissington villagers were kept in good health, due, they believe, to the pure water from the five local wells.

Just past the Coffin Well there's a fine duck pond, complete with a handful of ever-hungry ducks, but most eyes will be on the magnificent Jacobean hall. If it's closed to visitors, you can view it through the fine wrought-iron gates built by Robert Bakewell, or get an elevated view from the churchyard.

Tissington

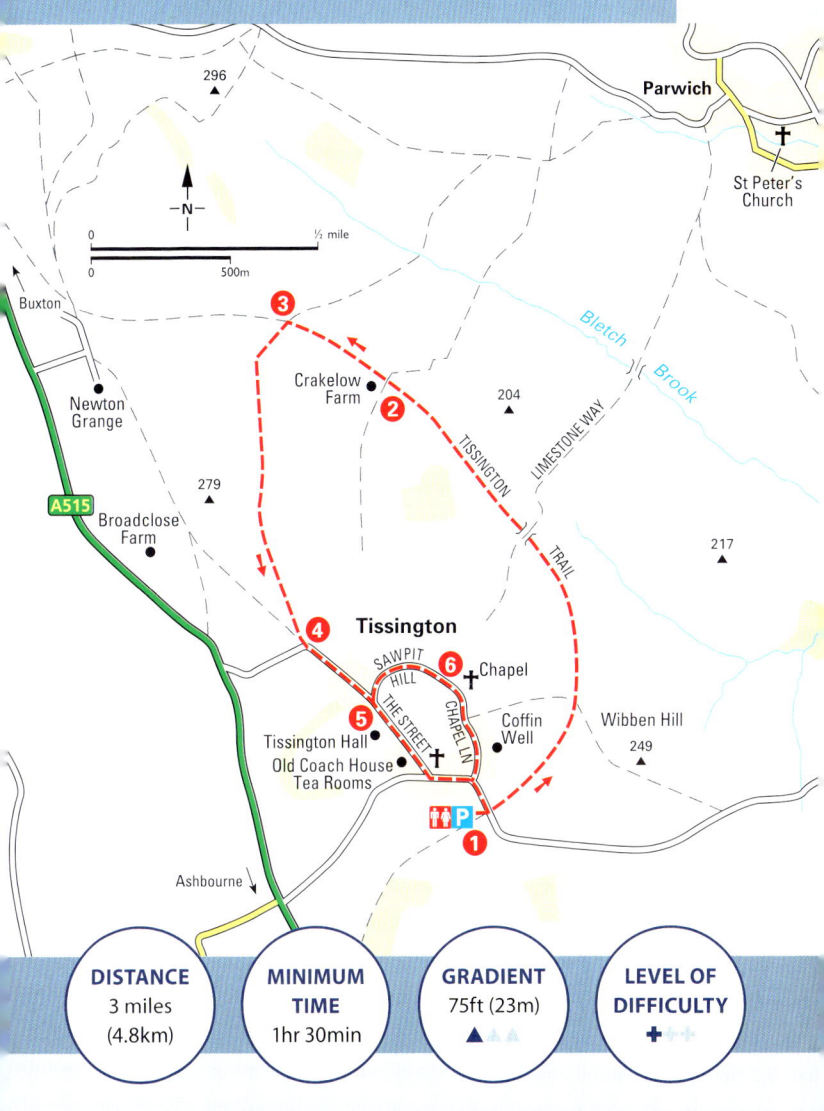

Walk 37

DISTANCE	MINIMUM TIME	GRADIENT	LEVEL OF DIFFICULTY
3 miles (4.8km)	1hr 30min	75ft (23m) ▲▲▲	✚✚✚

PATHS Old railway trackbed and field paths
LANDSCAPE Estate village and rolling farm pasture
SUGGESTED MAP OS Explorer OL24 White Peak
START/FINISH Grid reference: SK 177521
DOG FRIENDLINESS Good, but watch out for bikes on cycle trail
PARKING Tissington Trail pay car park
PUBLIC TOILETS At car park

Walk 37: Tissington

WALK 37 DIRECTIONS

❶ From the Tissington Trail car park follow the trackbed of the former Ashbourne–Buxton railway north-eastwards, signposted 'Tissington Trail to Parsley Hay'. Go under the bridge and steam on through the tree-lined cutting around the edge of the village.

❷ After 1.25 miles (2km) you reach the third overhead bridge since leaving the car park, with Crakelow Farm above. About 500yds (457km) further on you come to a clear stretch of trail where the trees vanish and there's a short embankment ahead, followed by a deep cutting. At this point, well-used footpaths lead off left and right.

❸ Go left, over a wall stile, signposted 'Public footpath to Tissington'. Make your way across the pasture to the top right-hand corner of the field. Now follow the wall on the right, which intermittently becomes a narrow walled track. Go over two further stiles and join a short farm track until you reach the road as it bends into Tissington.

❹ Go straight on, along a road called The Street, and then gently down towards the centre of the village past buildings.

❺ After 300yds (274m) turn left on to Sawpit Hill, a narrow lane, then turn right on to Chapel Lane to reach the Methodist Chapel.

❻ Beyond the chapel is Coffin Well, after which is a road junction. Turn right for the short walk past the duck pond to the tea rooms and Tissington Hall, or go straight on to return to the car park.

IN THE AREA
Tissington Hall was built by Francis Fitzherbert in 1609 to replace a moated manor house and has been home to the Fitzherbert family for more than 400 years. There are public tours and special events at certain times of the year.

EATING AND DRINKING
The Old Coach House tea rooms at Tissington serves coffee, lunch and afternoon teas, 10.30am–5pm. The Sycamore Inn at nearby Parwich is a community-run pub which also houses the village shop. For more mainstream fare, try the Bluebell Inn at the main entrance to Tissington on the A515.

ON THE WALK
Many of the regularly ploughed fields of Parwich and Tissington will have a few wild flowers in them, but take a look at the field-edges and the hayfields, for they will be rich in limestone-loving plants. In April and May, keep a watch for the increasingly rare cowslip (*Primula veris*). Its short single stem grows from a rosette of wrinkled leaves and its yellow flowers form a drooping cluster.

Dovedale

Walk 38

THE SOARING PEAKS OF DOVEDALE

Sample one of the Peak District's most dramatic dales and cross its famous stepping stones.

There are few dales in the Peak District with such a magnificent entrance as Dovedale. The River Dove squeezes through a narrow gap between Bunster Hill and the towering pyramid of Thorpe Cloud, guarding the narrow limestone valley like giant sentinels. You walk alongside the river at the foot of their steep slopes, variously covered with scrub, rocky outcrops and huge chutes of loose scree.

Pillars and Caves

Once through this gap, the river swings abruptly northwards and Dovedale is then characterised by luxuriant woodland, interspersed with sheer limestone cliffs, rocky pillars and caves. The dale bottom path is generally firm and level, allowing you to extend your outing quite easily. Further along are spectacular limestone towers like Tissington Spires and Ilam Rock, plus the intriguing Reynard's Cave high up on the eastern slopes. However, this walk goes as far as Lover's Leap, a bold rocky outcrop high above the river with a fine view across the dale to the pinnacles of the Twelve Apostles.

Stepping Stones

Although Dovedale is one of the most popular beauty spots in the Peak District, if you pick your moment and visit midweek, or early or late in the day, you can still enjoy the scenery and woodland in relative peace and not have to queue to cross the stepping stones. These iconic stones provide you with an optional return route along the far bank. They were originally built in Victorian times for visitors to Dovedale and thousands of people use them every year, but in 2010 Derbyshire County Council sparked controversy when they repaved the stones with mortared, limestone slabs. After many years' use the stones had become worn and uneven, often prone to flooding, making them sometimes difficult to use. There was criticism that the famous old stones had been sanitised and some of the thrill and challenge of crossing the river had been eliminated. You can judge for yourself as you negotiate the 17 or so stones – and whether you reach the other bank with your feet dry!

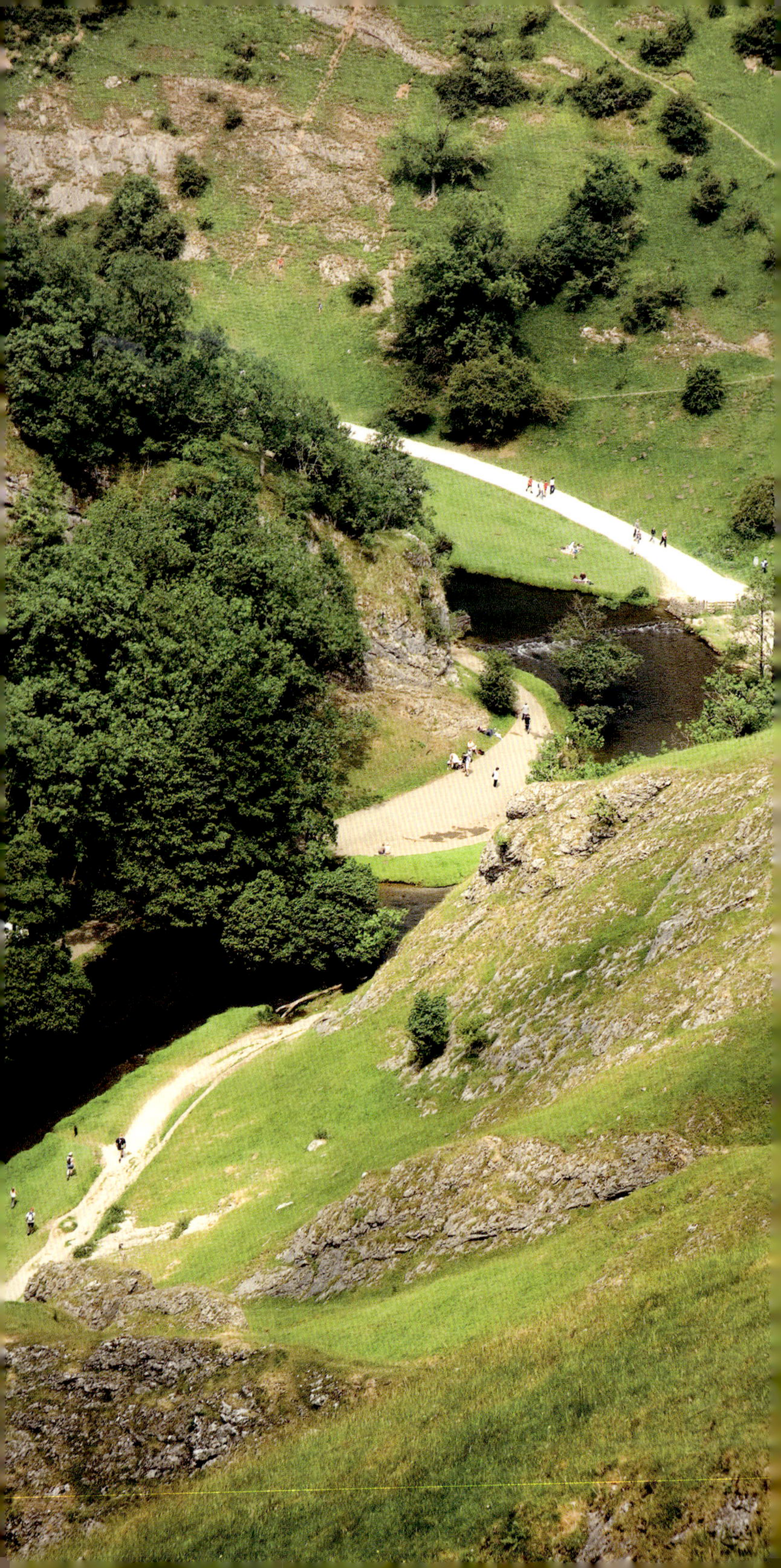

Dovedale

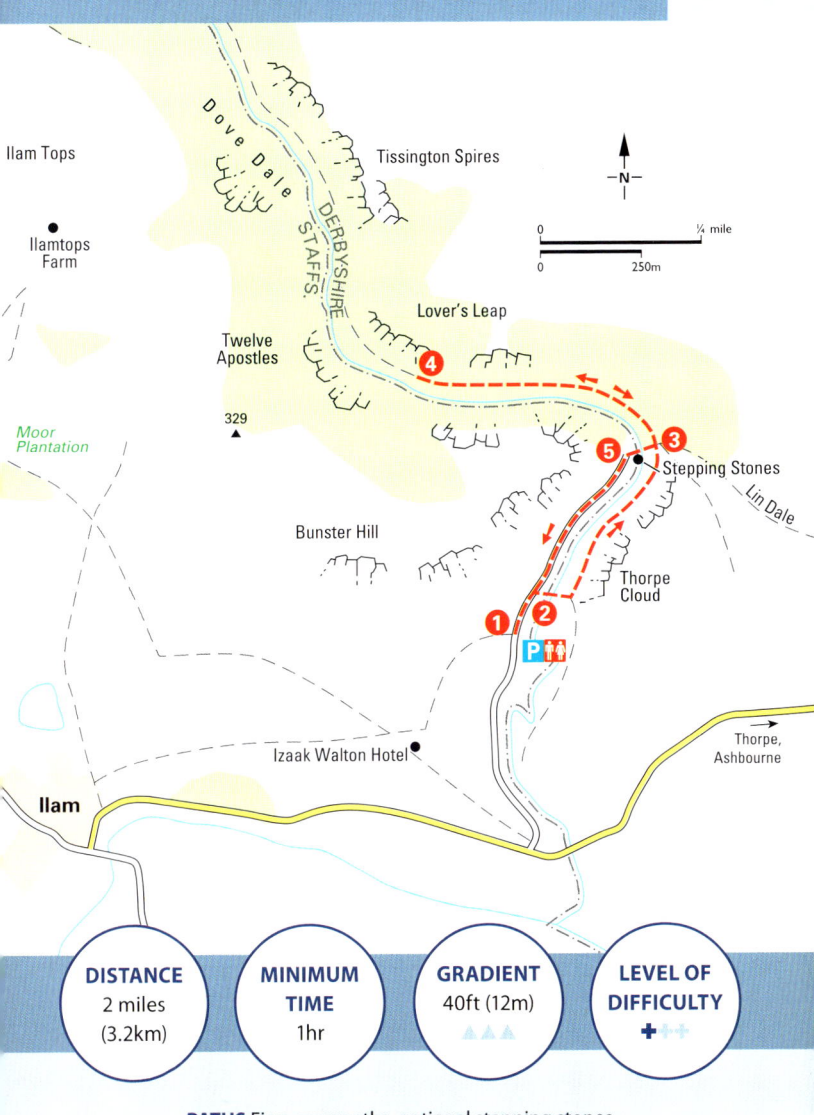

Walk 38

DISTANCE	MINIMUM TIME	GRADIENT	LEVEL OF DIFFICULTY
2 miles (3.2km)	1hr	40ft (12m)	

PATHS Firm, easy paths, optional stepping stones
LANDSCAPE Plunging, partially wooded limestone dale
SUGGESTED MAP OS Explorer OL24 White Peak
START/FINISH Grid reference: SK 146509
DOG FRIENDLINESS National Trust requests dogs under close control
PARKING Dovedale pay car park, near Thorpe
PUBLIC TOILETS At car park

Opposite: Dovedale is always popular with walkers

Dovedale 135

Walk 38 Dovedale

WALK 38 DIRECTIONS

❶ From the back of the toilet block at Dovedale car park follow the short path to walk between the river and the road. Soon you come to a long wooden footbridge, next to various information panels.

❷ Cross the footbridge and turn left. Walk along the foot of the steep slope on the path beside the river. When the river is high you may have to skirt the water's edge. Continue along to the stepping stones.

> **IN THE AREA**
>
> If you have the energy, it will be tempting to climb to the top of Thorpe Cloud. The sharp summit has wonderful views, both down the dale and across the expansive flatlands of the Midlands. The there-and-back path leaves the main route at Dovedale's meeting with Lin Dale, by the stepping stones.

> **EATING AND DRINKING**
>
> There's a seasonal snack bar by the car park, otherwise head for the Izaak Walton Hotel, a former 17th-century farmhouse near the entrance to Dovedale. The hotel's Dovedale Bar welcomes walkers and there's plenty of outdoor seating with great views across to Dovedale.

❸ If you want to scale Thorpe Cloud turn right here, otherwise go through the wall gap ahead and on along the wide, flat riverside path as the dale becomes wooded. Continue as far as Lover's Leap, where the path rises to a rocky promontory opposite the vertical limestone formations known as the Twelve Apostles.

❹ Turn round and walk back to the stepping stones, now framed by the immense bulk of Thorpe Cloud that towers behind. Cross the stones to the far side of the River Dove. If you would rather not cross the river via the stones simply retrace your steps to the footbridge along the south bank.

❺ Turn left and follow the wide, surfaced track all the way along the north bank back to the footbridge and on to the car park.

> **ON THE WALK**
>
> The steep slopes of Dovedale, most notably on Thorpe Cloud and Bunster Hill, have suffered from serious erosion. The effects of visitors scrambling up the sides have been compounded by rain and ice, resulting in long stretches of loose rock and scree. Temporary fences have now safeguarded the worst sections and shrubs and trees have been planted to stabilise the ground.

Ecton

Walk 39

DEEP MINES AND LIGHT RAILWAYS

Towering Ecton Hill was once famous for its copper and an odd little railway at its foot.

'A line starting nowhere and ending up at the same place' was one disparaging description of the Leek and Manifold Light Railway, a curious 8-mile (12.9km) narrow gauge line that had its northern terminus at Hulme End at the start of this walk. The line was opened in 1904 as a private concern and ran along the Manifold Valley to Waterhouses, where it joined the standard-gauge network. The station at Hulme End is now the Manifold Valley Visitor Centre and the engine shed a tea room.

Copper

You start by following the course of the line south into the narrowing Manifold Valley, then at Ecton you leave the railway behind and climb the steep hillside. It's time to turn your attention to what lies underground. Elsewhere in the Peak District the focus is on lead mining (see Walks 21, 31 and 35), but here at Ecton copper was the big prize. Both lead and copper mining had taken place here since early times, even before the Romans, but in the 1700s the scale of production really took off. Incredibly rich veins of copper were discovered and in 1786 the Duke of Devonshire's Ecton Hill mines produced about 4,000 tonnes of copper ore, reputedly making huge profits for the Duke which he used to help finance the construction of the opulent Georgian buildings of The Crescent in Buxton.

Ecton Hill

As you make your way up the steep, grassy slopes of Ecton Hill you'll notice that there are lots of fenced off shafts and the remains of former workings. The stand of pine trees above hides a giant spoil tip, for instance. Later in the walk you can look down at the pock-marked hillside from the top of Ecton Hill, which because of its important mining heritage is now a scheduled monument and a valuable educational resource. Because the copper deposits were found in vertical 'pipes', Ecton Hill contains the deepest mine in the Peak District. In fact, when it was dug in the late 18th century it may have been the deepest in the world at the time (over 1,800ft/550m deep).

Walk 39 Ecton

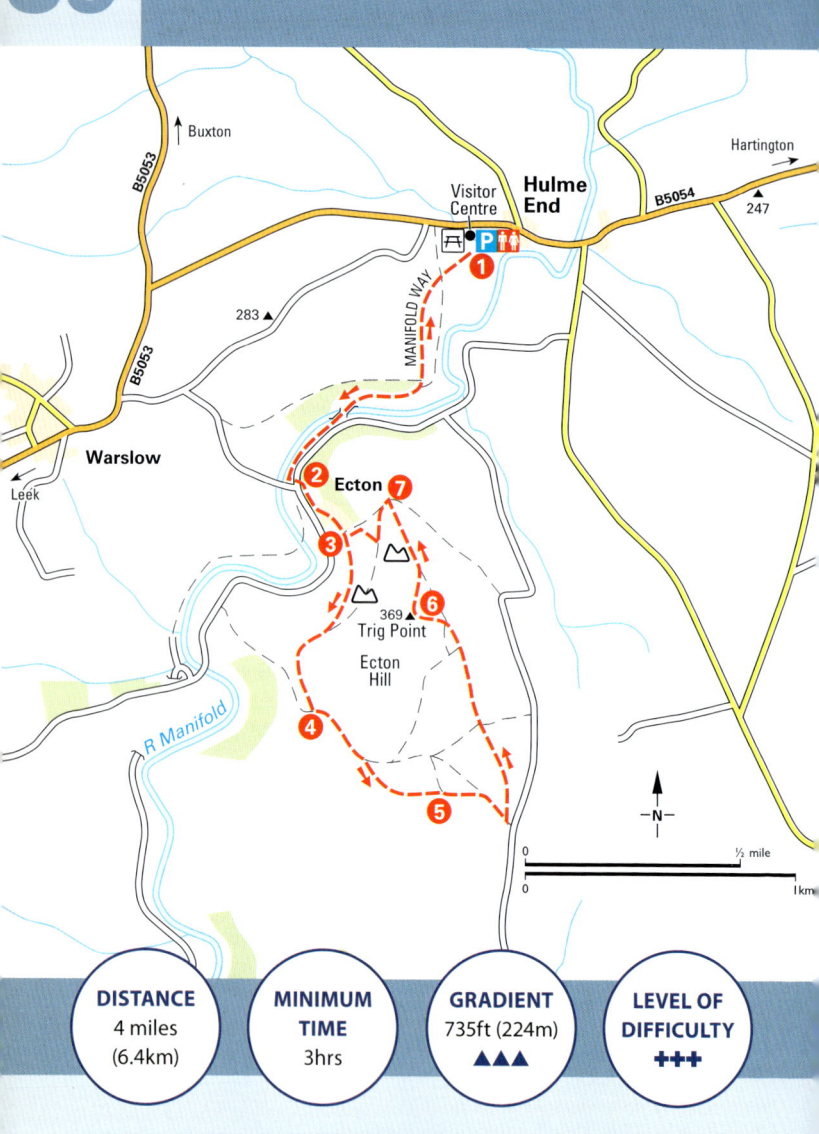

DISTANCE	MINIMUM TIME	GRADIENT	LEVEL OF DIFFICULTY
4 miles (6.4km)	3hrs	735ft (224m) ▲▲▲	+++

PATHS Surfaced tracks and grassy paths, some steep and slippery when wet
LANDSCAPE Narrow limestone valley with soaring hills
SUGGESTED MAP OS Explorer OL24 White Peak
START/FINISH Grid reference: SK 103593
DOG FRIENDLINESS Good on trail, but on lead around livestock in fields
PARKING Hulme End pay car park **PUBLIC TOILETS** At visitor centre next to car park **NOTE** Be careful around the open mining shafts on Ecton Hill

138 40 Short Walks in the Peak District

Ecton Walk 39

WALK 39 DIRECTIONS

1 Leave the car park on the Manifold Way southwards along the valley floor for 0.75 miles (1.2km). When you reach a road turn left, then at the junction go across another for the private road uphill, signposted 'Public footpath to Top of Ecton and Wetton'.

2 Go past several buildings, including the former mine manager's dwelling with its unusual copper-roofed spire. Beyond this the path continues between two stone sheds, under an archway, then over a stile on the left.

> ### 🍴 EATING AND DRINKING
> Next to the visitor centre at Upper Hulme is the Tea Junction, a café housed in the former engine shed of the light railway. Serving a tasty array of home-made food, both hot and cold, it's open Tuesday–Sunday April–September, and weekends at other times (closed December and January).

3 Turn right and follow the path out along the bottom of the slope. It gradually slants its way up across the steep, grassy hillside. Towards the top it levels out and at a line of hawthorn go up to cross a stile in the wall.

4 Walk across the field to the bend in a wall, then head half right. Go through the gate at the end of a line of trees and maintain your direction down across the next field, going over a drive. Cross the stile in the bottom corner and head left alongside the wall to reach a lane.

5 Go right and follow the lane uphill. Take the second path on the left, as the lane begins to descend. Go up the hillside close to the wall on your left. Continue straight on past a ruined building and aim for the trig point on the summit of Ecton Hill in view ahead.

6 From the top continue ahead, veering half right as the Manifold Valley appears far below to your left. Go through the corner of a broken-down wall to reach a gate in the wall below. Head down the hillside beside a wall until you reach a gate by a barn.

7 Don't go through the gate, but turn left, keeping the barn on your right. Walk across the hillside to the top edge of a crescent of pines, hiding an old spoil tip. From here take one of the zig-zag paths down the grassy slope to the bottom and turn right to rejoin the outward route.

> ### 🔍 IN THE AREA
> Although traffic was always light, the Leek and Manifold Light Railway did once serve a creamery at Ecton. This has long gone, as sadly has one at nearby Hartington much more recently. However, local cheeses are still on sale from the Hartington Cheese Shop in the centre of Hartington, including Dovedale Blue, a delicious soft blue-veined cheese.

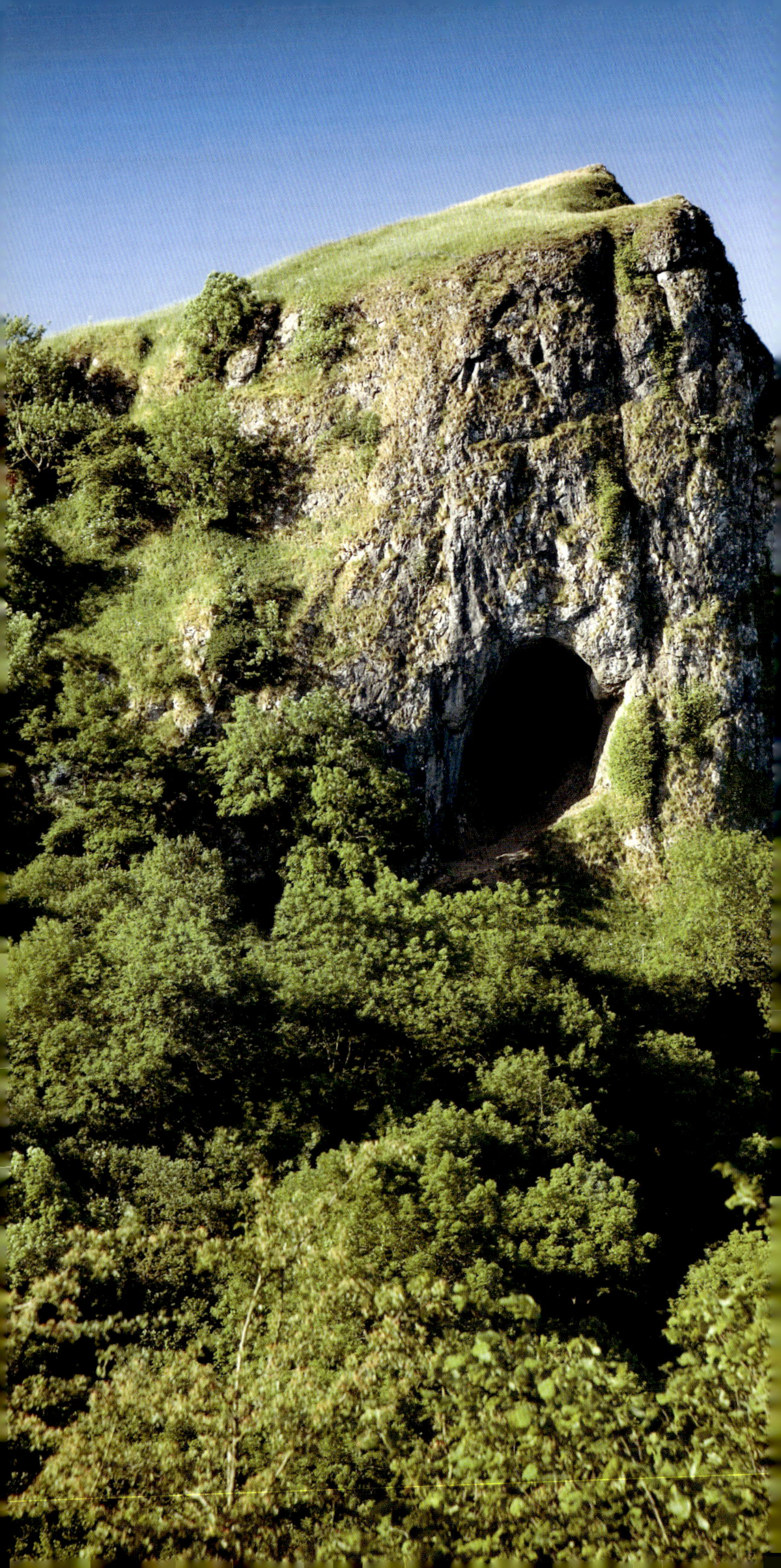

Grindon Walk 40

IN THE LAIR OF THE WHITE WORM

Follow a fascinating limestone trail to visit the film location of Bram Stoker's last nightmare.

Anyone who has seen Ken Russell's film, *The Lair of the White Worm* (1988), will recognise at once the entrance to Thor's Cave and may, as a result, feel slightly apprehensive when climbing the path up the hillside. The opening shot in the film features the famous landmark and, as the blood red titles roll, the camera slowly zooms in towards the mouth of the cave.

Scene of a Horror Film

Stoker's original story was based in the Peak District in the 19th century and tells of odd disappearances, legends of a fearsome giant serpent and of the strange and sinister Lady Arabella. Film maker Russell has moved the whole story in time to the 20th century and altered the plot considerably.
A young Scottish archaeology student, Angus Flint finds a reptilian skull at an excavation he's working on near his lodgings. Later he takes the two sisters who run the guest house to the home of Lord James D'Ampton for the annual celebrations to commemorate the slaying of the D'Ampton Worm by his ancestor. Angus leaves early to escort one of the sisters home.

Passing through woods near where her parents mysteriously disappeared they encounter the sensuous and snakelike Lady Sylvia. D'Ampton connects the disappearance of Eve with Lady Sylvia and, taking on his ancestor's role, heads for Thor's Cave to search for a tunnel connecting to Temple Hall.

Animal Lair

Thor's Cave may be the most famous cave in the Peak District but there are several others, including Ossom's Cave and Elderbush. Both have been explored and produced bones and flints from the Stone and Bronze Ages. So, Thor's Cave may have been home to one or two prehistoric beasties but in reality none of them were big white snakes. Formed over thousands of years from the combined effects of wind and rain on the soft limestone, it probably sheltered animals like giant red deer, bears or even early humans. Excavations have revealed it to be the site of a Bronze Age burial, although much of the evidence was lost by over-zealous 19th-century excavators.

Opposite: Thor's Cave in the limestone cliffs

Walk 40 Grindon

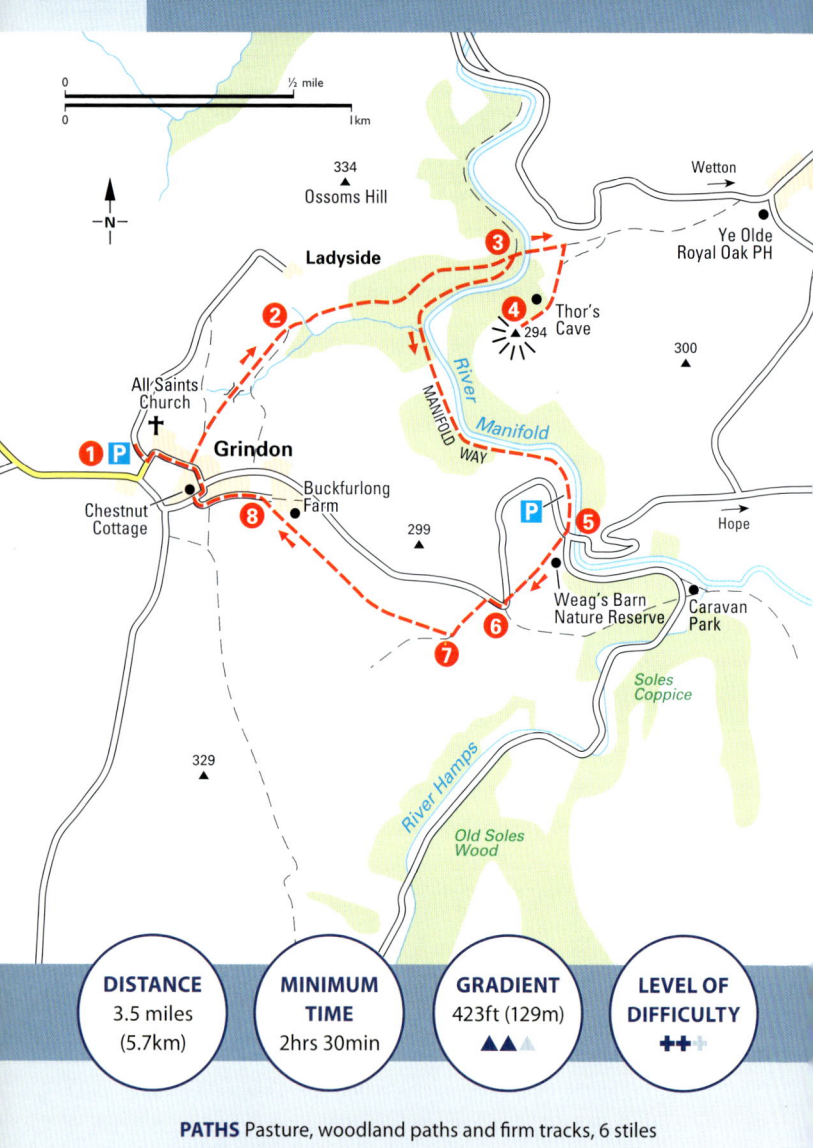

DISTANCE 3.5 miles (5.7km)
MINIMUM TIME 2hrs 30min
GRADIENT 423ft (129m) ▲▲
LEVEL OF DIFFICULTY ++ +

PATHS Pasture, woodland paths and firm tracks, 6 stiles
LANDSCAPE Hillside, valley, meadows and woodland
SUGGESTED MAP OS Explorer OL24 White Peak
START/FINISH Grid reference: SK 085545
DOG FRIENDLINESS Keep on lead near livestock
PARKING Car park behind Grindon church
PUBLIC TOILETS None on route, nearest at Waterhouses

142   40 Short Walks in the Peak District

Grindon Walk 40

WALK 40 DIRECTIONS

1 From the car park turn left, then left again by the playground and head downhill on the lane. After 150yds (137m) go left on to a public footpath, through a gap stile, cross a field and head downhill on the right of two diverging paths. Cross a bridge, go through a gate then a gap stile and go downhill, keeping the stream and the wood below on your right.

2 At the far end drop down to go through a wall gap on your right, continuing downhill into National Trust land at Ladyside. Cross over a stile, go through a wood and then leave it via another stile. Turn right, down the side of open pasture, then descend a winding path through trees to reach the Manifold Way.

3 Cross the Manifold Way, then a bridge and take the path uphill following the signs for Thor's Cave. At the mouth of the cave turn left, continue on a track uphill, curve right before a stile and follow the path to the summit for superb views along the Manifold Valley.

4 Retrace your steps to the Manifold Way, turn left and continue until you reach a car park. At its exit on to a lane take the footpath on the right, across a stile.

5 The public footpath heads diagonally left up the steep sloping hillside of Staffordshire Wildlife Trust's Weag's Barn nature reserve. Head for the top left of the field and continue up through the next.

6 At the very top go into the lane, turn left and then swing round the bend uphill. After 100yds (91m) turn left on to a gated bridleway. This soon dips downhill; at the bottom of the hill turn right on to a waymarked public footpath.

> **EATING AND DRINKING**
> From the summit slope of Thor's Cave, a footpath runs eastwards across the fields for just under a mile (1.6km) to Wetton. Ye Olde Royal Oak is located in the centre of the village and has long been a popular destination for walkers. The 400-year-old pub offers a choice of decent real ales, as well as hot and cold food served daily. If the weather is fine, you can sit outside in the beer garden and relax.

7 Keep straight on along the bottom of the shallow valley, maintaining your direction through successive fields, with the church spire at Grindon ahead. Keep to the left of the farm as you near the village.

8 Finally you reach a farm track. Turn left on to it and continue as it becomes a walled path, then turn right on to the road opposite Chestnut Cottage. Take the first left and follow this road back to the car park.

Walking in Safety

All these walks are suitable for any reasonably fit person, but less experienced walkers should try the easier walks first. Route finding is usually straightforward, but you will find that an Ordnance Survey map is a useful addition to the route maps and descriptions.

RISKS

Although each walk here has been researched with a view to minimising the risks to the walkers who follow its route, no walk in the countryside can be considered to be completely free from risk. Walking in the outdoors will always require a degree of common sense and judgement to ensure that it is as safe as possible.

- Be particularly careful on cliff paths and in upland terrain, where the consequences of a slip can be very serious.
- Remember to check tidal conditions before walking on the seashore.
- Some sections of route are by, or cross, busy roads. Take care and remember traffic is a danger even on minor country lanes.
- Be careful around farmyard machinery and livestock, especially if you have children with you.
- Be aware of the consequences of changes in the weather and check the forecast before you set out. Carry spare clothing and a torch if you are walking in the winter months. Remember the weather can change very quickly at any time of the year, and in moorland and heathland areas, mist and fog can make route finding much harder. Don't set out in these conditions unless you are confident of your navigation skills in poor visibility. In summer remember to take account of the heat and sun; wear a hat and carry spare water.

On walks away from centres of population you should carry a whistle and survival bag. If you do have an accident requiring the emergency services, make a note of your position as accurately as possible and dial 999.

COUNTRYSIDE CODE

- Be safe, plan ahead and follow any signs.
- Leave gates and property as you find them.
- Protect plants and animals and take your litter home.
- Keep dogs under close control.
- Consider other people.

For more information on the Countryside Code visit:
www.naturalengland.org.uk/ourwork/enjoying/countrysidecode